James J. Roche, Henry B. Carpenter

A Poet's Last Songs

James J. Roche, Henry B. Carpenter

A Poet's Last Songs

ISBN/EAN: 9783337265502

Printed in Europe, USA, Canada, Australia, Japan

Cover: Foto ©Thomas Meinert / pixelio.de

More available books at **www.hansebooks.com**

CONTENTS.

		PAGE
INTRODUCTION	. . . .	vii
THE POET-MAKER	. . . .	1
THE FOUR FUGITIVES	. . . .	3
THE PURPLE ASTER	. . . .	14
ANTITHETA	. . . .	18
PEARLS	. . . .	19
SIGHT	. . . .	20
THE END	. . . .	21
IN A WORLD LIKE THIS	. . . . . .	24
A LAMENT	. . . .	27
A TRIO FOR TWELFTH-NIGHT	. . . .	29
THE REED	. . . .	39
BEYOND THE SNOW	. . . .	44
THE SIRENS	. . . .	47
HOMESICKNESS	. . . .	49
PSYCHE	. . . .	51
THEODOSIUS	. . . .	54
A VACATION PRELUDE	. . . . . .	68
NON SINE LACRYMIS	. . . . . .	75
APOLLO	. . . .	78

	PAGE
THE WOODLAND STREAM	82
TRICHORDON	85
BENEATH HER FEET	87
KISSES AND TEARS	91
THE IMPOSSIBLE SHE	94
WHEN LOVE GROWS OLD	96
TOMORROW	100
AMERICA'S ANSWER	103
VIVE VALEQUE	105
SONNET	115
FRYEBURG	116
A NEW ENGLAND WINTER SONG	123
ODE TO GENERAL PORFIRIO DIAZ	126
ZEUS AND EUROPA	133
THE IDYL OF THE SPRING	142

HENRY BERNARD CARPENTER.

" Of manners gentle, of affections mild;
In wit a man, simplicity a child."

*Such was Henry Bernard Carpenter, a man born
with the gifts of song and eloquence, endowed with ripe
learning, admired and loved by all who knew him; yet,
to the end of his days, a simple, kindly, unspoiled child of
Genius. Goldsmith himself was not less worldly-wise than
this, his latter-day countryman, brother poet and almost
counterpart in body as in mind.*

*He was born in Dublin, Ireland, on April 22, 1840.
His father was a clergyman of the Established Church.
On the mother's side the poet was descended from the
Boyds of Derry, a family distinguished for intellect and
courage. The clergyman dedicated his three sons to his
own profession. The two who survive are Rt. Rev. Wil-*

liam, Bishop of Ripon and ex-Chaplain to the Queen, and Rev. Archibald, Rector of Bloomsbury, London.

Henry, the eldest son, was sent at the age of eighteen to Oxford University, from which he graduated in 1862, as exhibitioner, honor man and prize man. In the following year he was appointed a master in Portora Royal Collegiate School, the "Eton of Ireland." Among his pupils were Oscar Wilde and his brother Willie. In 1864 he was ordained chaplain of the school, subsequently accepting the position of chaplain to the Earl of Belmore and his tenantry. Although eminently successful as a teacher, all his tastes turned towards the field of letters. He wrote many poems which attracted the attention of cultivated readers. He was a natural orator and readily found admiring audiences, but the material rewards were insufficient to meet his modest desires and he resolved to seek a wider field in the United States. Accordingly, in 1874, he sailed for America, encouraged by a hope, which was not destined to be gratified, of obtaining a professorship in Bowdoin College, Maine.

He made his first appearance on the platform at Quebec, but as he was comparatively unknown and unheralded, he met with but little success. Thence he crossed the border to Maine and lectured for a charitable benefit at Fryeburg, a lovely little town on the Saco, the praises of which he has sung in his poem, " Fryeburg."

The talents of the young minister were quickly recognized. He was offered the pastorship of the Congregational Church at Bridgton, and accepted the position, filling the pulpit and also the pews by his marvellous eloquence, during a period of four years. He had declined a flattering offer from an Independent church in Portland, but the fame of his oratory spread abroad and in 1878 he accepted a call from the trustees of Hollis Street Church, Boston, to fill the pulpit made illustrious by a long line of noted divines, from Mather Byles to Thomas Starr King.

He fulfilled the duties of his new pastorate with marked success during ten years. The church had languished before his coming, as the march of business had encroached upon the residences in the neighborhood. Mr. Carpenter's eloquence did not suffice to stay the progress of trade, but it brought back the parishioners, and the old church took on a new lease of life under his ministry.

His genius soon won him recognition outside of his congregation. He had made his mark as a public speaker before coming to Boston, filling lecture engagements not only in Maine but throughout the country and Canada. His subjects covered a wide range, historical, poetical, philosophic and political. The enumeration of their titles alone would fill many of these pages. He was that rare thing, an eloquent extempore speaker. He never attempted to write out and memorize his addresses. With the barest outlines of fact, date and suggestion, to guide him, he would clothe his glowing thoughts in language so well-chosen, polished and vigorous, that a verbatim report of his words would need scarcely a single erasure or alteration. It was a fatal facility, for it relieved the orator of the necessity of writing his speeches ; and so they are lost to the world forever. But one or two of all his addresses have been reported with any degree of fulness, and they have lost

rather than gained by the newspaper writer's paraphras-
ing. This is the more regrettable, as both are on patriotic
American themes, and on such he was always ardently
and sincerely eloquent.

But wide and varied as was his range of oratory, he
was never so fervidly inspired as when treating of his
native land. Grattan, O'Connell, Sheridan and all the
great men of his race were the especial subjects of his
marvellous periods. All that brought honor to his coun-
try he honored and loved, with no narrow limitations of
class or creed. The Celtic spirit was introduced into nearly
all his public discourses. With characteristic simplicity
and earnestness he took his place, a few years ago, primer
in hand, to learn in a Gaelic school the rudiments of the
language which he loved for its traditions.

The literary world of Boston was not long in discover-
ing the worth of this unobtrusive poet, among the first to
perceive the hidden talent being his countryman, John
Boyle O'Reilly, always keenly alive to any merit which
might bear the Celtic stamp. A friend invited him to at-

*tend one of Carpenter's lectures, and he was at once
enchanted. At the conclusion he went up to the platform
and introduced himself to the orator. Thenceforward the
two were friends. O'Reilly invited Mr. and Mrs. Carpenter to be the guests of the Papyrus Club at the ap-
proaching "Ladies' Night." Shortly afterwards, Mr.
Carpenter was elected to membership, and remained to the
day of his death one of the best beloved sons of Papyrus.
There his kindly heart and gifted mind were appreciated
as nowhere else, save at his own fireside. Elsewhere his
superiority might provoke the envy of Philistine or Phar-
isee, to his injury and pain; but the refined Bohemia saw
what was best and greatest in him and judged him there-
by. His finest poems were first read at its board, the
lightest-hearted pausing to listen when, with the indescrib-
able thrill of tenderness in his sweet, mellow voice, he would
adjure :*

"Step lightly, Mary, for my heart's beneath your feet."

*He was also a popular member of the St. Botolph, the
Round Table and other Clubs, a welcome guest at every*

drawing-room reception of literary and social Boston, and a courtly, genial host in his own home. He had been married during his sojourn at Bridgton, to Miss Emma Bailey, daughter of Captain R. T. Bailey of that place. With his wife and only child, a handsome boy of seven, he went on a year's tour to the Mediterranean, in 1887, visiting Greece and Italy and coming home with a fresh, rich store of classical treasures. On his return he gave two successful courses of lectures, illustrated with views of Greek scenery and architecture, and was preparing for an extended lecture tour throughout the country when death cut short his brilliant career.

The end came almost without warning. He had suffered for some time from varicose veins and had been compelled to remain in his room for several days. He was spending the summer with his family at Sorrento, Maine. On the evening of July 16th he entertained a party of friends and retired to bed apparently in good health and spirits. On the following morning he arose, and was in the act of dressing himself, when he suddenly fell back-

ward and almost instantly expired. A clot of blood from the congested vein had flown to the heart, and though medical assistance was immediately summoned, nothing could be done for his relief. The warm heart had ceased to throb, the gifted brain was dead, the eloquent tongue was silenced forever.

The following pages contain the shorter lyrics which their author was preparing for publication during the last months of his life. His noble long poem, "Liber Amoris," was published by Ticknor & Co., of Boston, in 1887, and achieved an immediate success, passing through several editions. The rare melody of these lyrics, their exquisite finish, their rich imagery and many strong, heroic passages, prove that Henry Bernard Carpenter was truly a poet, as he was truly an orator of the first rank.

His eloquence, alas, remains like the sweet notes of a great singer, only a memory in the ears of those who listened to his voice. He left no manuscripts of his speeches, for, as I have said, he prepared nothing. Even the fine oration delivered before the City Government and citizens of Boston on the Fourth of July, 1883, though subsequently printed by the City, was not reported verbatim and loses all its beauty in the version which, he naively says, " was prepared from my notes and the newspaper reports, after the Fourth of July."

Happily the world has not lost his beautiful lyrics. The poet remains, though the orator's voice be silent. Dearer than either, remains the memory of the Man, simple, frank, kindly, generous in thought and word and deed. Peace to his gentle spirit !

JAMES JEFFREY ROCHE.

THE POET–MAKER.

"POETA NASCITUR, NECNON FIT."

Once a little song I made
In a garden as I strayed,
On the myrtle leaves in morning dew I traced it;
But by noontide not a line
Found I of that song of mine,
Where the finger of the sunbeam had effaced it.

Then in scorn of self I laughed,
And forswore the Poet's craft,
And I turned from Love, the Poet's lord and master,
Yea, I turned and fled away,
But he followed me all day;
When I fled, he always followed me the faster.

Bow and arrow had he none,
But his looks were like the sun,
And his lips two founts of fire that flowed together,

He had wings of crimson grain,
Bright with pleasure, dark with pain,
And the tempest of his flight no god could tether.

From those wings he plucked a plume
And he pressed its point of doom
To his lips, where sleep the rosy-cradled kisses,
Back his weaponed hand he drew,
Aimed, and cleft my heart in two.
Oh, when Love selects the mark, he never misses!

Then I wept. But Love said, "Write."
So I drew that plume to light
Streaming redder from the heart he just had smitten,
And I wrote, and learnt with years,
That on parchment washed with tears
And in heart's-blood every poem must be written.

THE FOUR FUGITIVES.

I.

On a clear glad April morn
    Youth, a boy-babe, took his seat
On an ancient dial worn
    With the Sun-God's fiery feet.
    Crownwise on his brows were set
    Primrose, maybloom, violet,
    And the coming summer skies
    Glowed in locks and cheeks and eyes.
    On the shadow-haunted dial
    Forth he drew his airy viol,
    Stroked its strings, unlocked its heart
    Lifewards, and thro' each quick part
    Strange sweet sounds began to creep,
    Softer than the soul of sleep,
    Till the dial's journeying shade
    Smote his thigh, — like one afraid,

Up he leaped, nor more he played,
But with frowns of dark denial
Down he dropt from off the dial,
Quenched his song, and quelled his viol,
And, for all that I might say,
Shadow-struck, fled fast away;
While I cried, " Ah! welladay!
      Stay, oh, stay."

I I.

In Love's garden next I stood
    Mid the myrtle's green increase,
Where great roses red as blood
    Dreamed their passion into peace.
From his mansion marvellous
Made of amorous apple-boughs, —
Whose soft slow blush-tinted showers
Knolled the noiseless-footed hours, —
Forth came Love, a shepherd lad,
Star-eyed, ruddy-limbed, unclad,
Bringing flower-wine of his valleys
In a sorrow-charming chalice,

Spiced with myrrh and magic root.
Straight I drank : the while his flute
Gurgling loosed my speechless grief,
And, as streams that win relief
For the o'erbrimming mountain mere,
When it sheddeth tear by tear ;
So my passioned thought came borne
Down those sliding sounds forlorn,
And I cried : " Love, stay with me.
Here forever would I be
In thy garden thus with thee."
" Nay," said he, " for in these valleys
Others crave my song and chalice."
So he passed beyond his palace,
And, for all that I could say,
Bore his love-notes thence away,
While I wept, " Ah ! welladay !
　　　Stay, oh, stay."

III.

Faint for love, I found a dell,
　　Whose green twilight said in sooth,

"Here lives one will heal thy hell,
    Love's calm sister, maiden Truth."
In this dell no love-notes yearned,
No love-flowers looked up and burned,
But a fountain's musical tone
Rose in swiftly-various moan.
Seemed it, Thought's unfancied fleetness,
Joy's own sadness, Grief's own sweetness,
Hope and laughter, sighs and tears,
Love, Birth, Death, Time's fluent years,
Fate and Memory, — all were found
In that myriad-mingling sound.
And the fountain-stone showed red
With the life of them that bled,
Who each year unsealed the well,
And, unsealing, deathward fell.
With one cup of orient water,
Up rose Truth, the fount's pure daughter,
Naked, and her body was
Soft as dew and clear as glass, —
Naked, yet half-hid from sight
In a robe of woven light,

Which, in sky-assurgent stream,
Like some heaven-returning dream,
Upward grew, and fold by fold,
In its mist of gradual gold,
Veiled her eyes of tearful blue,
Where Love's dayspring trembled through.
"Drink," she said, "and dream and die,
All are dreams beneath the sky;
Drink, 'tis all I give thee now,
More the Gods may not allow;
Seek me still and keep thy vow."
Then, as Youth, whose very fleetness
Matches Love's own incompleteness,
Sank this water-visioned sweetness,
And, for all that I could say,
Fountain-hid, flowed fast away;
While I moaned, " Ah! welladay!
      Stay, oh, stay."

IV.

" There's no balm for broken hearts,
    There's no light for darkened homes,

None to wipe the tear that starts,
 Until Time the Healer comes.
 So I sighed, while now my way
 Westward sloped with fall of day,
 And I came and sat alone
 On the mile's last sculptured stone.
 Soon from spoiled lands, like morn's ray,
 Rushed a steed foam-flanked and grey,
 Lighting-reined, a thing of wonder,
 Maned with storm and hoofed with thunder,
 And a strong man sat thereon,
 In whom Age and Youth seemed one,
 From whose golden mouth this chant
 Rang to the hoofs reverberant, —
 "I bring balm for broken hearts,
 I wipe every tear that starts,
 I pour light thro' darkened homes,
 I am Time: thy Healer comes."
 "Stay," said I, "stay then awhile
 In this daylight's dying smile."
 Whereto he: "Hadst thou at morn
 Asked me this, I had forborne.

Now thy prayer claims no defence;
See, night comes, and I must hence.
For with morn's first hours I creep,
Swifter course with noon I keep,
But tow'rd night I bound and leap."
Wild as childhood's dream of wonder,
Flashed he thence on hoof of thunder
Down the valleys darkening under,
And for all that I could say,
Fast and faster fled away;
While I wailed, " Ah ! welladay !
        Stay, oh, stay."

V.

Then I cried and sighed to be
    Where the unfleeting visions are,
Till Heaven called for Night, and she
    Led God's thoughts forth, star by star;
    And an onward-beckoning hand
    Led me to a waste low land,
    Stemmed with growths of silent gloom, —
    Funeral yewtree's hearselike plume,

Hermit poplar's heavenward tress
Sighing up its loneliness,
And weed-nurturing sylvan spaces
Thick with whispering fears, the places
By old Night's pale people trod,
Demon, fay and forest-god.
There She met me in mid path,
Who the keys of Aiden hath.
O'er her gloomed a cypress-wood,
And behind her, like a hood,
A large moon of mellow rim,
Showed her white face warm and dim,
Showed her heavy hyacinth hair,
Spread in clusters burnished fair,
Eyes fixed on the eternal Now,
And clear throat and eyes and brow,
Like proud marbles of the Greek
Great with woes they will not speak,
Then two snowy slopes of breast
Round their vale of tearless rest,
And a sable robe's downfall
Wet with tear-dew shed by all.

There with hands behind her drawn
Stayed she me. A doubtful dawn
Of new life dwelt in her face,
A constraining regal grace
Crowned that look, which, as a spur,
Goads the world to question her.
So I spake to her and said :
" Summoner of the quick and dead,
Thou who holdest in thy hands
All these darkened valley-lands,
Shadow-stoled Persephone ;
Say (for all things flow to thee)
Harbourest thou in thy pure clime
Life's defaulters, — healing Time ;
Slow-paced, softly-speaking Truth ;
Star-eyed Love ; and sun-haired Youth ; —
Those who wooed me scarce a day,
Won my faith and fled away ;
Though I cried, " Ah ! welladay !
            Stay, oh, stay."
Whereto, gentle as a child,
She replied in accents mild :

" They that met thee on thy road
Hold on earth no fixed abode,
Sent as shadows where ye dwell,
Pilgrims from the Invisible ;
But their substances unspent
Dwell where all is permanent."
Then with white arm drawn apart
From the side where beats man's heart,
Hollowed she a sunlit space
Deep within her calm embrace ;
As a stooping silver birch
Flanks a wood-path, when we search
Down its dusk to where the day
Floods the arched walk with its ray.
There, beneath life-laden trees,
Bowing o'er their psalteries,
Sang the young-eyed seraphim,
Green-couched by a fountain's brim,
With blown hair that flamed above
Rapture-lifted mouths of love,
And wide wonder-lighted eyes
Lost in smiles of deep surmise.

And in midst of these there stood
That fourfold Beatitude
Round about a grassy throne,
With white blossoms overblown,
Like the Prophet's mystic Four
Seen in Patmian cave of yore
Chanting " Holy " evermore.
And I saw bright sylvan spaces
Sown with flowerlike forms and faces
Of the dead world's happy races,
Whilst, like thunder far away,
Rose a spheral roundelay
From the Four who thus did say :
  " Here, we stay."

THE PURPLE ASTER.

[In parts of New England this flower is known by the
name of Farewell-Summer.]

Oft have I thought that o'er the gleaming
    Golden-eyed flower of the marguerite
There passes, amid her nightly dreaming,
    Transfiguration strange and sweet ;
That breathing away her soul in payment
    She takes the empurpled autumn air,
And weaving thence new heavenly raiment,
    Comes back to life as the Aster fair.

Or again I have thought in wayside musing,
    That I saw in the flower's upturned eye
The hills' deep violet interfusing
    With gold of the summer's fading sky ;
As though a drop of the sun, forgetting
    Its birthplace far at the noonday's height,
Had fallen and framed for itself a setting
    In starry rays of sapphire light.

But throughout all such fleeting trances,
    One thought returns at each period.
Through every mood this flower advances,
    Sill ushered in by the Golden Rod
To Flora's court, the sweet last comer,
    Rich drest, as a herald, going between
Winter half-wakened and waning summer,
    'Twixt what is coming and what has been.

O last of the freeborn wildflower-nation !
    O last in the hedgerow here to-day !
Three names are thine, and they fit thy station,
    Each making known in its simple way
Winter at hand, thine overcomer ;
    Thy bright hours gone ; and thy starry crest ;—
There is Frost-Flower, Aster, and Farewell-Sum-
    mer,
    But Farewell-Summer suits thee best.

Sad Flower ! on thy lips we lay the burden
    Of that sad word we cannot say.
Thou comest with short late life for guerdon,
    To mourn for the summer passed away,

Through Nature's grief-hushed voice invited
  To stand by the perished flowers of the dell,
By the forest's funeral pyre new-lighted
  And speak the thrice-wailed word Farewell.

Frayed and pinched by the frost's first fingers,
  Thou waitest unpitied, poor and lone,
As one who the welcome of life outlingers,
  Scarcely counting himself his own.
Not one tired bee, one golden hummer,
  To soothe thee to sleep with droning spell,
Alone thou sighest, O dear dead Summer,
  And all that is Summer's, fare you well.

As Apollo wrote, while his woe flowed faster,
  His sad "ai ai" on the hyacinth leaf,
So for dead Summer, O mourning Aster,
  Thy purple is pale as with silent grief.
Love no more, and yet Love remembered,
  Is the tale which thou, and they can tell,
Who sigh over hope's last fire low-embered,
  O Love's lost summer, for aye farewell.

A path unfinished, with nothing thorough,
    Is the way of life, if I deem aright,
'Twixt little hope and a deal of sorrow,
    'Twixt heaven and hell, 'twixt day and night,
'Twixt arrows out of the darkness darted,
    Hints of a coming winter frost,
And dreams of a summer time departed,
    A glory vanished, an Eden lost.

O golden-eyed, sky-purpled Flower,
    In the silent sunlight born to shine!
O fellow-heir to an equal dower!
    Our lots are the same, both thine and mine;—
To come upon earth, a short-lived comer
    Between a morning and evening bell,
To wake between winter and waning summer,
    To see the world and to say, — Farewell.

ANTITHETA.

Ἐκ τῶν ἐναντίων καλλίστη ἁρμονία.

— *Aristotle.*

Lo, Death and Sorrow and Pain are sweet,
    And Life and Pleasure and Joy are good,
And these are one and as one shall meet,
    When all we feel shall be understood.

Then lift thy face unto Sorrow's rain,
    Yea, deem it sweet as the spring's young
      breath,
Stoop low and drink of the pool of Pain,
    Dip thy Life's urn in the well of Death.

For Bliss is painlike, and Pain is bliss,
    And Love must weep till the dawn of day.
Then Death shall waken at Life's warm kiss,
    And Joy wed Sorrow in smiles for aye.

PEARLS.

Say not : I never throw to fool or clown
  My goodly pearls ; for swine I ne'er amassed
    them ?
Say rather : Are these pearls which I cast down
  And are those always swine to whom I cast
    them ?

SIGHT.

Man in his sorrow sees more clear
Through the crystal of one little tear,
Than if the whole air, as a spy-glass, should
Draw Heaven into nearest neighborhood

THE END.

All is as the end is.
Those were thy words, part of the street-learn'd lore
    Garnered by thee and murmured mid the hum
    Of Stamboul's throughfares, O Chrysostom,
Heaven's blameless beacon by the Bosphor shore,
    Golden-mouthed angel of Byzantium !
All is as the end is.
Forth, ye muezzins on your minarets,
Where Prayer still bows and pays her evening
    debts,
Cry ye to man when man all hope forgets ;—
        Say : All is as the end is ;
Call no day dark or bright till the sun sets.

All is as the end is.
What train is this that threads the staring street ?
    Whom do they circle with such circumstance ?
    Pass they to court, or nuptial feast, or dance ?

Thine eyes, O Chrysostom, are turned to greet
   The pageant, while thou say'st in thoughtful
     trance, —
       All is as the end is.
Oft one foul deed a whole fair life o'ersets.
Caught in the law's inextricable nets,
For yon poor wight his blade the headsman whets,
       Then all is as the end is.
Call no day bright or fair till the sun sets.

       All is as the end is.
Again low-murmured from thy golden tongue
   We hear the self-same words, when through
     the din
   And darkness of thy city's shame and sin
Thou cam'st, as guest, thy feasting friends among,
   Where at the threshold sang thy heart with
     in, —
       All is as the end is.
No more for his past pains the feaster frets,
When at the song-soothed feast he smiles and wets
In red wine the rose-wreathen coronets.

Then all is as the end is.
Call no day dark or drear till the sun sets.

All is as the end is.
What of dark days if evenings be serene?
The Past, the Past makes not our destiny,
But that which in the Future still we see.
Man is not always what he once has been,
But rather what he hopes and strives to be.
All is as the end is.
Duty may spring from pangs which Grief begets
And Life's best purposes from dead regrets,
Like scent distilled from vanished violets.
For all is as the end is.
Call no day dark or bright till the sun sets.

IN A WORLD LIKE THIS.

In a world like this,
When in misanthropic,
    Cheerless mood, I wis,
    Tired I take my flight,
Far from Love's warm tropic, —
    Then I fret and sigh :
    Better 'tis to die
Than to fawn and follow
    With false look submiss,
    Meeting day and night
Heartless hearts and hollow,
    In a world like this.

In a world like this,
Trade's a daily duel,
    If your aim you miss ;
    And I hear them say :
" Woods are made for fuel,
    Not for poets' nooks,

Day-dreams, birds and brooks ;
Bees are but for honey ;
For our gospel is,
Seek the things that pay,
Make not men but money,
In a world like this."

In a world like this,
How the sleek saints palter !
Give the Iscariot's kiss
With the blessed wine
Poured upon Christ's altar !
Measure Man by rules,
Shut up God in schools,
Sound with three-foot plummet
Life's and Death's abyss,
Call their lore divine —
Egoists consummate
In a world like this !

In a world like this . . . !
Yet, when I remember

All the love and bliss
Showered on man from May
Down to Life's December,
Beauty beyond odds,
Banquetings with Gods,
Mornings with Apollo,
Nights with Artemis;
Then I answer, Nay,
All's not hard and hollow
In a world like this.

A LAMENT.

Now is the time of tears and sighs
    (Roam, sad heart, roam.)
When dark rains fall and loud winds rise,
And grief lives in the lips and eyes.
Beauty has faded from the skies.
    The honey-bee's gone home.

Wan flowers, your happy life is spent.
    (Roam, sad heart, roam.)
Far is the wing that o'er you went
With hum of brooding deep content,
Feeding your souls with song and scent.
    The honey-bee's gone home.

What life shall now your lives renew?
    (Roam, sad heart, roam.)
Gone is the mouth which brought for you
Love-tidings from all flowers and drew
Your treasured sweetness, as its due.
    The honey-bee's gone home.

Come, Darkness, this is now thine hour.
　　(Roam, sad heart, roam.)
Rise, ye wild winds, with storm and shower,
Rend every leaf from autumn's bower ;
Lie there, Hope's last forsaken flower.
　　The honey-bee's gone home.

A TRIO FOR TWELFTH-NIGHT.

I.

Who first brought man the morning dream
Of a world's hero ? Whence the gleam
Which grew to glory full and sweet,
As the wide wealth of waving wheat
> Springs from one grain of corn ?
What drew the spirits of earth's grey prime
To lean out from their tower of time
Tow'rd the small sound of Hope's far chime
> Heard betwixt night and morn ?

First it was sung by heaven ; then scrolled
By the scribe-stars on leaves of gold
In that long-buried book of Seth,
Which slept a secret deep as death,
> Unknown to men forlorn,
Till a seer touched a jasper lid
In a sand-sunken pyramid,
And out the oracular secret slid,
> Betwixt the night and morn.

Zarathustra, Bactria's king, next said :
"When in the sky's blue garden-bed
A lily-petalled star shall fold
A human shape, the gift foretold
        Shall blossom and be born :
Then shall the world-tides flow reversed,
New gods shall rise, the last be first,
And the best come from out the worst,
        As night gives birth to morn."

II.

So while the drowsed earth swooned and slept
Mute holy men their vigils kept,
By twelve and twelve : as light decayed,
They marked through evening's rosy shade,
        The curled moon's coming horn,
All stars that fed in silent flock,
And each tossed meteor's back-blown lock.
So watched they from their wind-swept rock,
        Betwixt the night and morn.

Slow centuries passed ; at last there came
By night a dawn of silver flame,

Whose flower-like heart grew white and round
To a smooth, perfect pearl, with sound
      Of music planet-born,
In whose clear disk a fair child lay,
And " Follow me," was heard to say :
Round him the pale stars fled away
      As night before the morn

Forthwith from morning's crimson gate
The Three Kings rode in morning state
Across Uläi's storied stream,
With westward wistful eyes agleam
      As pilgrims westward borne,
They left the tide to sing old deeds,
The stork to plash half-hid in reeds ;
A thousand spears, a thousand steeds,
      They rode 'twixt night and morn.

III.

Melchior had coat and shoes of red,
   And a pure alb sewn with gold thread;
Beneath a tire of Syrian mode
Streamed the soft storm of hair that snowed

From cheek and chin unshorn ;
Down to the ground his saffron pall
Fell as warm sunbeams earthward fall,
And he, sun-like, seemed king of all,
      Betwixt the night and morn.

Red-robed, red-sandalled, golden-clad,
Came Gaspar, beardless as a lad :
Through his fair hair's divided stream
His red cheeks glowed as poppies gleam
      Through sheaves of yellow corn.
Love's life in him was scarce fulfilled,
Like as, when daybreak shadows yield,
Night's iron lids lie half unsealed
      In colors of the morn.

Bronzed Balthasar, with beard thick-fed,
Came last, in tunic royal red
And broidered alb and yellow shoon.
With him life's rose had touched its noon,
      And died and left the thorn, —
Which proved by its sharp, thrilling heat
That larger life is less complete

Till the heart's bitter grows to sweet,
    As night melts into morn.

IV.

Said Melchior, "In blue silk I fold
The rock's best fruit, red-hearted gold :
So grant us, mighty Mother East,
One who shall raise thy power decreased,
    And break Rome's pride and scorn,
Till our red, wine-warm world hath sent
Its breath through the cold West, and blent
The Orient with the Occident
    In one wide sea of morn."

Said Gaspar, "I bring frankincense
From Caraman's hills, whose thickets dense
Hide the balm-bleeding bark which feeds
The fuming shrine with fragrant seeds :
    So may this child, when born,
Be Love's high Lord, and yield his love
As incense, and draw down the Dove
To crown his brows in sign thereof,
    Betwixt the night and morn."

Said Balthasar, " And I bring myrrh,
In death and life man's minister;
Which braves decay as burial-balm,
Or, mixed with wine, brings the deep calm
    Which power and love both scorn :
Such be this child, — God's answering breath
To the one prayer the whole world saith,
'Oh, grant us myrrh for pain and death,
    Betwixt our night and morn.'"

V.

Twice fifty sennights o'er them bent
The fierce blue weight of firmament.
Through sea-like sands they still pursued
The unsetting star, until it stood
    Above where, travail-worn,
A new-made mother smiled, whose head
Lay near the stalled ox, as she fed
Her babe from her warm heart, on bed
    Of straw, 'twixt night and morn.

As day new-sprung from dropping day,
Near her in shrining light he lay,

And made the darkness beautiful.
Couched on low straw and flakes of wool
  From Bethlehem's lambs late-shorn,
He seemed a star which clouds enfold,
Swathed with soft fire and aureoled
With sun-born beams of tender gold,
  The very star of morn.

At her son's feet the kingly Three
Laid, with bowed head and bended knee,
Their gold and frankincense and myrrh,
Nor tarried, — so the interpreter
  Of God's dream once did warn, —
But hied them home ere the day broke;
While without awe the neighbor folk
Flocked to the door, and looked, and spoke,
  Betwixt the night and morn.

VI.

A tall centurion first drew near,
Brass-booted, on whose crest sat Fear.
He bent low to the fragrant bed,
With beard coal-black and cheek rust-red,

And each palm hard as horn ;
Quoth he, "Our old gods' empire shakes,
Meherculé ! Now this babe o'ertakes
All that our Venus-Mother makes
    Betwixt the night and morn."

A shepherd spake : " Behold the Lamb,
Who ere he reign as heaven's I AM
Must undergo and overcome,
As sheep before the shearers dumb.
    Unfriended, faint, forlorn.
Him then as King the skies shall greet,
And with strewn stars beneath his feet
This Lamb shall couch in God's gold seat,
    And rule from night to morn."

A woman of the city came,
Who said, " In me hope conquers shame.
Four names in this child's line shall be
As signs to all who love like me, —
    God pities where men scorn :
Dame Rahab, Bathshebah, forsooth,
Tamar, whose love outloved man's truth,

And she cast out, sweet alien Ruth,
  Betwixt the night and morn."

Next Joseph, spouse of Mary, came, —
Joseph Bar-Panther was his name, —
Who said, " This babe, Lord God, is thine
Only begotten Son divine,
  As thou didst me forewarn ;
And I will stand beside his throne,
And all the lands shall be his own
Which the sun girds with burning zone,
  And leads from night to morn."

Said Zacharias, "Love and will
With God make all things possible.
Shall God be childless ? God unwed ?
Nay ; see God's first-born in this bed
  Which kings with gifts adorn.
I would this babe might be at least
As I, an incense-burning priest,
Till all man's incense-fires have ceased,
  Betwixt the night and morn."

Whereat his wife Elisabeth :
" My thoughts are on the myrrh, since death
Shades my sere cheek, which, as a shore,
Is wrought with wrinkles o'er and o'er.
      Now be this child new-born
A prophet, like my prophet-boy, —
A voice to shake down and destroy
Throne, shrine, each carved and painted toy,
      Betwixt the night and morn."

But Mary, God's pure lily, smiled :
" Lord, with thy manhood crown my child, —
More man, more God ; for they who shine
Most human shall be most divine.
      Of those I think no scorn,
King, prophet, priest, when worlds began ;
But higher than these my prayer and plan ·
Oh, make my child the Perfect Man,
      The Star 'twixt night and morn."

THE REED.

"ET ARUNDINEM IN DEXTERA EJUS."

Beneath the memnonian shadows of Memphis,
  it rose from the slime,
A reed of the river, self-hid, as though shun-
  ning the curse of its crime,
And it shook as it measured in whispers the
  lapses of tide and of time.

It shuddered, it stooped, and was dumb, when
  the kings of the earth passed along.
For what could this reed of the river in the
  race of the swift and the strong, —
Where the wolf met the bear and the panther,
  blood-bathed, at the banquets of wrong?

These loved the bright brass, the hard steel,
  and the Gods that kill and condemn;
Yea, theirs was the robe silver-tissued, and
  theirs was the sun-colored gem;
If they touched thee, O reed, 'twas to wing
  with swift death thy sharp arrowy stem.

Then the strong took the corn and the wine,
    and the poor, who had scattered the seed,
Went forth to the wilderness weeping, and
    sought out a sign in their need,
And the Gods laughed in rapturous thunder,
    and showed them the wind-shaken reed.

O dower of the poor and the helpless! O key
    to Thought's palace unpriced !
When the strong mocked with cruel crimson
    and spat in the face of their Christ,
When the thorns were his crown — in his faint
    palm this reed for a sceptre sufficed;

This reed in whose fire-pith Prometheus
    brought life, and the arts began,
When Man, the God of time's twilight, grew
    godlike by dying for Man,
Ere Redemption fell bound and bleeding,
    priest-carved to the priests' poor plan.

Come hither, ye kings of the earth, and ye
    priests without pity, draw near,

Ye girded your loins for a curse, and ye
builded dark temples to Fear,
Ye gathered from rune-scroll and symbol great
syllables deathful and drear.

Then ye summoned mankind to your Idol, the
many bowed down to the few,
As ye told in loud anthems how all things
were framed for the saints and for you, —
" Lord, not on these sun-blistered rocks, but
on Gideon's fleece falls thy dew."

Man was taken from prison to judgment ; a
bulrush he bent at your nod ;
Ye stripped him of rights, his last garment,
and bared his broad back for the rod,
And ye lisped, as he writhed down in anguish,
" This woe is the sweet will of God."

But lo ! whilst ye braided the thorn-crown
for Man and the children of men,
Whilst ye reft him of worship and wealth, and
he stood mute and dazed in your den,

A reed-stalk remained for a sceptre; ye left
in his hand the pen.

Sweet wooer, strong winner of kingship, above
crown, crosier and sword,
By thee shall the mighty be broken, and the
spoil which their might hath stored
Shall be stamped small as dust and be wafted
away by the breath of the Lord.

His decree is gone forth, it is planted, and
these are the words which he spake, —
No smouldering flax of first fancy, no full
flame of thought, will he slake,
No bruisèd reed of the writer shall the
strength of eternities break.

Behold your sign and your sceptre. Arise,
imperial reed,
Go forth to discrown king and captain and dis-
inherit the creed ;
O strike through the iron war-tower and cast
out the murderer's seed ;

Go forth —- like the swell of the springtide,
  sweep on in measureless sway,
Till raised over each throned falsehood, in
  bright omnipresence like day,
Thou shalt bruise them with rod of iron and
  break them like vessels of clay.

BEYOND THE SNOW.

Bare boughs ; athwart each suppliant arm
    The sun's pale stare at pale November,
No autumn's amorous breath to warm
    His red last leaf's expiring ember ;
      House after house, a glimmering street ;
      A herald grain of coming sleet ;
      The struggling dayfires' lessening glow ;
      Hour when light ghost-winds wailing go,
    When men least hope and most remember,
    Before the snow, before the snow.

A village cot ; eyes fiery-blue,
    Blithe voice beneath the roof's high rafter,
Ripe cheek, crisp curls of chestnut hue,
    Quick heart that leaps to love and laughter,
      That feeds on all from star to sod,
      And loving all things lives in God ;
      Light feet borne daily to and fro
      On some sweet errand none may know,

Swift sped with hopes like wings to waft her
 Along the snow, along the snow.

A midnight room ; the smothered speech
 Of those that watch with tear-stained faces ;
The helpless love-look bent by each
 Who stoops, but speaks not, and embraces ;
  Love braving Death with that last cry,
  " She is mine, she is mine, she shall not
   die ; "
  Then homeward steps returning slow
  To the great tear's unworded woe,
 And many darkened dwelling-places,
 Across the snow, across the snow.

A hollow grave ; and gathered there
 Strong breaking hearts that bear and break
  not,   ˙
Round the closed eyes and lifeless hair
 Life's few that follow and forsake not ;
  Tears, the drink-offering to the dead,
  The bruised heart's grape-wine softly shed ;

Long downward looks ; they will not go,
They fain would sleep with her below,
In dreamless rest, with those that wake not,
Beneath the snow, beneath the snow.

A green plot sweet with shade and sound,
A white porch and a name engraven,
Where Death unveiled as Love sits crowned
In garden-lawns with lilies paven,
And she a daughter of that land,
A silent rose in her right hand,
And in her left a scroll where glow
Mysteries of might, which man shall know
In Love's warm-shadowed leafy haven,
Beyond the snow, beyond the snow.

THE SIRENS.

ON DE BEAUMONT'S PICTURE "LES SIRÈNES."

Dainty sea-maids! bright-eyed Sirens! laughing
over dead men's graves!

What has drawn you from the inland to this wilderness of waves?

Why those lucent arms uptossing o'er your should-
ers round and rare?

Why those musical throats bent back beneath the
sunlight of your hair?

Oh, the bosoms' rosy treasures tempting tow'rd
their fragrant home!

Oh, the ivory thighs unkirtled on the white flowers
of the foam!

Bitter is the sea about you with the brine of daily
tears,

In the sea-grave lie beneath you withered hearts
and wasted years.

Back! ye deathward-singing Sirens! One by Gali-
lee's calm sea

Calls you hence, — " O cease your angling,
    drop your nets, and follow me,"—
Calls you home to Love's high service in seclu-
    sion's holy glen,
But he never called you shoreward to be fishers
    after men.

HOMESICKNESS.

I knew a strong man,
And he dwelt mid the hills where the swift streams
    ran,
For he loved to live where his life began.
But they took him away, and made him abide
Where the great streets darken and chafe and chide
    With their ceaseless tide,
And he mourned for the hills which mourned for
    the man,
    So he sickened and died.

I knew a weak bird,
And she sang in the woods where her song was
    first heard,
For she loved the bowers by her young wing
    stirred.
But they caught her away, and made her abide
In a cage where she sang not, but often cried
    For her lost forest wide,

And she mourned for the woods which mourned
    for the bird,
      So she languished and died.

      O Land of the Soul!
Men have lived on thy hills within Love's control,
And fain had they stayed where thy star-streams
    roll.
But a hand plucked them thence and made them
    abide
In a world where they wandered, and often cried
      For that first hillside, —
"O Love, take us back to thy Land of the Soul."
      So they sorrowed and died.

PSYCHE.

Love came to me one morn in May,
Bringing all glad things on his way,
"Lo, here are Autumn and Summer and Spring,
All three seasons in one I bring."
 He spake me smooth,
 And he sware for sooth,
That his gold was good, and his troth was truth.
 Alack, the day !
 Heigho, Sing Sorrow !
Man sows in vain what he reaps with pain,
And the joy once gone shall be never again
 Heigho, Sing Sorrow !
 'Tis ever thus
 Love deals with us ;
Builds his bower for to-day, and then flies away
 To-morrow.

I gave him all in my garden's girth,
Myrrh and spices and balms of worth —
My side was the couch wherein he sank,

My heart the warm cup whence he drank.
    Where the basil grows,
    I culled the rose,
And wrapped him in myrtle-shadows close.
       Alack, the day!
    Heigho, Sing Sorrow!
Man sows in vain what he reaps in pain,
And the joy once gone shall be never again,
    Heigho, Sing Sorrow!
      'Tis ever thus
      Love deals with us;
Builds his bower for a day, and then flies away
      To-morrow.

I woke one morn at the end of May,
And Love rose up and went his way,
And all the guerdon I can win
For the love I laid at his feet, has been
    A handful of rue
    Wet with grief's dew
And sad-eyed pansies, just a few.
      Alack, the day!
    Heigho, Sing Sorrow!

Man sows in vain what he reaps in pain,
And the joy once gone shall be never again.
    Heigho, Sing Sorrow!
        'Tis ever thus
        Love deals with us ;
Builds his bower for a day, and then flies away
        To-morrow.

THEODOSIUS.

All things are beautiful that God hath made, —
Green earth, skies grey or crimson, sheen or shade,
The golden river-dust, the mid-sea slime,
The mold-warp's home, and hills the throne of
    Time,
Rich dawn, with thrush, and saffron-flowering reed,
And darkness, friend of death, and worm and
    weed.
Shadows of silence, and great lights of sound
Alike are dear to th' heaven they float around,
And God hath blest them, whether in field or
    flood,
In earth or air, and called them very good.
But ere these leave the arms of their kind Nurse,
Man clothes them with the garment of his curse,
And driving out with flame-sword, seraph-wise,
He disinherits them of their Paradise.
'Tis the old story of the scapegoat still,
We lay on other lives our self-wrought ill ;

Man points at Woman, Woman at her feet,
"The Serpent tempted me, and I did eat."

In the far East, as story telleth us,
Dwelt the great Emperor Theodosius,
By the rough Thracian strait, where Io roamed
Salt fields of sea, wind-fretted and o'erfoamed.
All power was his, the king's twain-handed might,
And Life, and Law, and all, save sacred sight.
But, God be praised, the chance that seals one
      sense,
Stays not the whole flow of man's providence.
So at his palace door a bell he hung,
Which, when it woke him with its iron tongue,
Cried ever in his ear, " O Sire, descend,
And give me justice, and be misery's friend."
Then would you hear the shuffling, sightless feet
Which brought him to the hall and judgment seat,
Where he sat down, this Emperor Theodose,
And sentence gave 'mid his magnificoes,
So the world sought him as some isle o' the sea,
Where men breathe rights and all the men are free.

Now fell it on a day when Spring's new flame
Pricked bird and flower and leaf, a serpent came
And built her home and stowed her innocent
    freight
In a green plat, hard by the palace-gate,
And there she dwelt, a helpless, harmless thing,
With sweet, strange mother-love encompassing
And coiled in sleep about her little ones,
As God's vast life rings round his stars and suns.

One morn, while absent from her dear abode,
There came with short, light leaps, a songless toad
Through thickening grass-plumes, to the serpent-
    nest,
Where her brood lay just sleep-warm from her
    breast,
And swallowing these, his body burdensome
He straight lay down in that unchilded home.
Swift came the serpent-mother back again ;
One glance around, then fierce with deathlike
    pain,
She flashed straight at the murderer of her joy,

God-armed with right to cast out and destroy.
Not yet : for oft the Gods are kind to guilt,
And fools grow fat where the pure blood lies spilt.

Driven out, this creature, childless, exiled, poor,
Slow wound her weak folds to the emperor's door,
Where, gathering all her battle-broken strength,
She flickered up and writhed her sliding length
Round the smooth bell-rope tow'rd the speechless
    bell,
Which drawing down, she woke the summoning
    knell,
" Descend and give me justice." Straight uprose,
And took his seat, that Emperor Theodose,
Saying, " Go, bring him hither," and one came
In black velure and taffeta robe of flame,
Peeping with outstretched neck and watery laugh,
Who smote the snake thrice with his ivory staff,
And switched her from the grunsel, and returned.
Scarce had the sightless Theodosius learned
From the cold courtier's tongue the serpent's
    crime,

When hark ! the bell knolled out the second time,
" Descend and give me justice," and to end
The full appeal, it rang once more, " Descend."

   Then called the blind king to his seneschal,
A reverent man, of face angelical,
With love-lit eyes, voice musical and low,
White hair and soft step like the falling snow :
" Hie thee, and fetch this thing whatso it be ;
Who doeth kind deed, the only king is he."
And with soft step the senior went, and found
The stricken serpent half-way to the ground,
And caught her well-nigh dead, reft of all hope,
Failing through faintness from the throbbing rope,
And bore her, inly pitying her woes,
And laid her down before King Theodose.

   O then, I ween, a work right marvellous
Was wrought of Him, who somewhere teacheth
    us, —
Certes, all things are possible with God.
Yet men will say in time's last period,
This was not so, these tales are light as sand,

Faith-forged in Jewry or old Grecian Land, —
Not knowing how in antique days, by oak
And fountain, beasts and birds together spoke,
Under the forest's shadow-woven tent,
In session sage and peaceful parliament;
Till Man came, and henceforth from bird and beast
The primal word's divisible language ceased,
And so to place their thoughts above our reach,
They chose their free-born, inarticulate speech.
Yet sometimes these, when heavenward raised by
    wrong,
Change cry for speech, as men change speech for
·   song ;
Or, as when Slavery's bow at Man is bent,
Man cries to God, and then is eloquent.
Nor count it strange that He who once came down
In tongue of fire to be the Prophet's crown,
And shook his soul as with the rushing South,
Should ope in one brief speech a serpent's mouth.

So with raised head the serpent thus began :
" Smite me, but hear.   I come to thee, O Man ;

For unto thee, they say, the seat is given
Of Mediator-God 'twixt us and heaven.
In thy sere autumn, when hopes fade and fly,
Thou yearnest upward to the listening sky,
And criest and sighest and sayest, ' Lord, how
    long ? '
To some one, whom ye call the Sweet and
    Strong —
What that one is to thee, art thou to us,
Girt with great strength and knowledge glorious.
Shall Mercy drop to thee her royal meat,
Who keepst her crumbs from them that kiss thy
    feet ?
Think not, great king, that we, who roam and
    range
Wild ways of life which teach us uses strange,
Are aliens to what makes the best in men,
In soldier, statesman, sire and citizen, —
The lover's anguish dipt in tides of death,
Child-trust, and mother-love that fashioneth
All thought and thew, life's prodigality
That breathes the noble rage to save or die ; —

These which are ours we share with thee, O Man,
In Life's wide palace cosmopolitan.
Hear me. There came a toad into my nest,
Whiles I was absent on a needful quest,
And killed my pretty brood, and now he keeps
That home from her, who at thy footstool creeps.
Full well I know that something just and good
Ere many suns will give me back my brood,
But give me now the lair which is mine own, —
Guard my ground nest, and I will guard thy
    throne."

Long mused the blind king Theodosius,
But when at last his heart full piteous
Sent its red message to his cheek, he spake : —
" Ah me ! sad woes ye bear for human sake,
Poor hunted lives, beast, bird and creeping thing,
From Man who is your brother, not your king.
But chiefly on thy head that lies thus low
Have we laid down the weight of all our woe.
Give ear and hear me, my most honored lords,
And you, ye learned clerks, wise in your words,

Stand forth and answer me : Who first decreed
Discord for all things sown of mortal seed?
Who blew through earth the ban of civil war
Which flames above us, reddening Arés' star?
God, will ye say ? Heaven wot, that cannot be.
Hear Nature's *Miserere Domine*
Go up, man-scorned, an awful litany
Folding the feet of God with folds of moan,
And crying, Our eyes look unto Thee alone.
Not God. Who then ? Ye durst not answer.

'Tis Man, who blots her fountain, slays her tree,
Blasts her pure river, tears her breast of green,
And calls her beasts now clean, and now unclean
Lowering her names of serpent, ape and dog,
To suit the sins of man's own catalogue ;
For through man's heart distil those drops of gall
Which must o'erflow and on some creature fall.
O dull of spirit and cold of heart to make
This cleanser of the dust, the earth-loving snake,
The authoress of your ills, the fount of sin ;
Forgetting in your doctrines' battle-din,

How God ordained that, since the world began,
Each thing in turn should be the friend of Man.
·What! shall the Lamb that healeth all of us
Tread on the Snake of Æsculapius?
Say, are not innocent Wisdom and wise Love
Wedded for aye — the Serpent and the Dove?
O sweet Lord Christ, when thou didst come on
    earth,
Thou mad'st the stall of ox thy bed of birth;
When in chill desert thou didst leave our feasts
To share Life's hunger, thou wast "with the
    beasts";
When on to Zion Town they saw thee pass,
'Twas not on war-steed, but on lowly ass;
And when to win us worlds by thy self-loss
Thou didst lift up for us the bitter cross,
Then didst thou take the thorns we oft had cursed
To be thy crown, of all great crowns the first.
Help me, dear Christ, in pity thus arrayed
Like thee, to love all things which God hath made.
So Pain shall school me into sympathy,
And what I should have been, I yet shall be."

Then Theodose sent one from all the rest
To reinstall the serpent in her nest,
Who came and finding there the murderer
Crushed him and cast him out ; and some aver
That from the bruised head of the loathly thing
There oozed a sea-green gem, forth issuing ;
Wherefore and how it boots not here to tell, —
Certes, with God all things are possible.

After these things it fell on a bright day
Near the calm shut of eve, this blind king lay,
Wrapped in his purple, gold-embroidered pall,
And slept a space in the same palace hall,
When lo ! a thing most rare was brought to pass.
As though new-raised in beauty from the grass
That serpent through the palace came again,
No more updrawing her loose length with pain,
But glittering like a stream with rains fresh-dewed,
Amber, and silver-mooned, and rainbow-hued,
Eyed like a moist large planet of the South
That shines a promise of rain in days of drouth.
So swept she glorying up the porphyry floor,

And in her mouth a bright great emerald bore.
Therewith, (but whence it came none ever knew,)
Through all the house a wondrous music grew,
Such concords as are heard from voice and string
At heavenly doors by spirits first entering, —
Immortal airs, touches of mellow sound
That came in long-drawn sighs, above, around,
And march-like music swoln to mighty tone,
Like preludes from aërial clarions blown,
And whispers as of multitudinous feet,
Which died away with waifs of scent most sweet.

Soul-charmed, the serpent tow'rd King Theo-
    dose crept,
And there she hung above him, as he slept
With silent face, and silent, pale dead eyes
Turned in, as 'twere, on Life's mute mysteries ;
Then, as the downward-swaying branch lets fall
Its shining fruitage to the lips that call,
So she soft-stooping o'er his sleep, unknown, —
Dropt on his eyes the magic emerald stone.

Meanwhile blind Theodosius dreamed a dream.

In the high heaven he saw a coming gleam,
Which brightening as it came to where he lay,
Opened at last like the full flower of day.
It was God's angel, strong Ithuriel,
Armed with that glowing lance, which, sooth to
    tell,
Unlocks all doors of light in earth or skies,
With whose bright point he touched the sightless
    eyes,
And said, "Receive thy sight;" thus much he
    spoke
And vanished, and King Theodose awoke.

Opening his new-born eyes he looked abroad,
Oh wonder! Oh the beautiful earth of God!
He gazed on the rich picture, fresh and fair,
The grateful fields of green, and liquid air,
But first tow'rd heaven and its blue gulfs of sky.
What sees he there? Up through long glades of
    light
God's city rose upon his trancèd sight,
Pillar and palace built of mist and gem,

And sun-clad wall of New Jerusalem,
Where men walk free from sin and terror and
    tears,
With smile sent back on time and passèd years,
Then, as the pageant faded from his eyes,
He watched beneath its vanishing traceries
The dawning eventide of one faint star
And lilac cloud's flame-bordered bank and bar,
And lower down, the green wood's tender gloom,
And lawns that fed on dews and balm and bloom,
Whilst, like a meteor, through his palace door
The serpent shivered and was seen no more.

A VACATION PRELUDE.

[At Athens, on the second day of the Eleusinian festival, the candidates for the Great Mysteries assembled, and waited for the well-known words of the Hierophant or Mystagogue. At the cry, "To the sea, ye initiates!" (hálade mústai), they rose and went down to the shore, where they received baptismal purification, and thence proceeded to the temple of Demeter (the Earth-mother) at Eleusis, to be initiated in the greater or final Mysteries of life and death.]

" Hence to the sea ! souls true and tried,

Plunge in the Gods' baptismal tide !

Thence to Demeter's temple-stair

And learn Life's deeper secrets there ! "

The Prophet speaks ; they hear the call,

They rise and leave thy sacred wall,

Thy homes and haunts of sweet renown !

Queen City of the Violet Crown !

Onward with heart-kept vows they creep

Round the grey, olive-shaded steep —

Through ways that beckon lovingly

Down to old Ægeus' fabled sea ;

That sea that shines and shakes afar,

Inlaid with many an island star,

Poseidôn's bright, rock-jewelled band
Clasping his loved, lost Attic land.

" Hence to the sea ! " that cry once more
Comes, organ-voiced, from surf and shore,
Comes through the hum and hurrying feet,
The toil and tumult of the street.

From each dull brick I learn the call
Flashed as from old Belshazzar's wall ;
Market and church and street and store
Echo the mandate, " To the shore ! "

With Care's sharp thorn-wreath daily crowned,
Our wave-girt city hears the sound,
And stoops with toil-worn diadem
To touch the healing Ocean's hem ;

And take new strength from him who erst
With his waves rocked her, swathed and nursed,
Who now with blue, large, wondering eye
Hails her, his Venice throned on high.

" Hence to the sea ! " the summons came
O'er fields adust, down skies of flame ;

I heard, and fondly turned to thee,
O gentle, glad, all-gathering Sea!

I saw thee spread but yestermorn,
As though for Venus newly born,
A couch of satin soft and blue,
O'er which the sun-showers dimpling flew.

To-day how changed! the loud winds rise,
The storm her sounding shuttle plies,
Weaves a white water-shroud beneath,
And all the sea-marge answers, " Death."

Through sheeted spray what sights appear!
Faces look out and shapes of fear;
Mad through the trampled surge abroad
Revels and reels the Demon-god;

Whilst o'er his shouts that wax and wane
Swells one long monotone of pain,
As o'er some city's rabble yell
Tolleth a great cathedral bell.

Is this the deep-sea peace I sought?
Calm days by holy shores of Thought,

Airs, that might Hope's own clarion fill
With tones divine of " Peace, be still " ?

And yet to me these tides that flow
Are but as clouds o'er worlds below,
Worlds which look up to skies, as we
Look to our heaven's o'erhanging sea.

Not on that sea-floor, but beneath
Its snowy shroud and funeral wreath
Peace dwells.   What kingdoms calm, and fair,
And changeless, greet my guesses there !

Seeds of the New that is to be
Sleep in the ooze of yon grey sea;
Life, Love, all strange and speechless things,
To crown the heart's imaginings, —

Rich hills, green-skirted, forest-zoned,
Cliffs on which slumbrous Powers are throned,
High-pillared shades, with splendor laned ;
By ruthless woodman unprofaned ;

Close-latticed lights, cool shadowings,
And murmurs of all pleasant things,

Fountains that chime away their cares
In liquid lapse down crystal stairs ;

Glades which a tender twilight fling
Like the green mist of groves in spring ;
Blameless white sands, and seas of pearl,
Where young-eyed Dreams their sails unfurl ;

Doors opening from afar with tone
Of mystic flutes in musings lone,
Low chantings thrilled through dim-lit seas,
Old harp-notes, half-heard prophecies ;

Pale temples veiled in sapphire gloom
Where the great ghosts of glorious doom
In transport list, till heaven-born Fate
Shall ope her Sire's tremendous gate ;

Caves where the gentle, gracious Hours,
Who bring all good things, weave strange flowers,
And faint Hopes wait in Lethè grots,
Brow-bound with fresh forget-me-nots ;

Genii, low dwellers of the glen,
And souls forlorn that shall be men,

Mute lips that once have kissed the wrong,
Which time shall purge and light with song;

Strong angels, waiting for the day,
When they shall shoulder seas away,
And show to God new blessed hills
Starred with undying daffodils;

When Earth, with bridal morning strewn,
Like a pure goddess grandly hewn,
Shall, re-baptized and born again,
Rise from her centuries' trance of pain.

Thus in thy heart, O Deep, are stored
Kings' treasure-chambers, unexplored;
Thy terrors, tumults, fears are found
But on thy surface, in thy sound.

"Hence to the sea!" I heard that call,
And left the world's loud palace-wall
To find thee, O thou vast Unknown,
By shores of mystery and of moan.

Yet, nameless Dread, that seem'st but so,
Calm are thy depths of peace below ;
Roll dark or bright, O Spirit Sea,
Why should I fear to sink in thee ?

NON SINE LACRYMIS.

It was that hour when vernal Earth
And stormy March prepare
For the first day of April's tearful birth,
That I, o'ercome with care,
Rose with the twilight from a fireless hearth,
To take the fresh first air
And smile of morning's mirth.

Tired with old grief's self-pitying moan,
A mile I had not strayed,
Ere my dim path grew dark with double zone
Of men full fair arrayed,
While blent with sound of battle-trumpets blown,
Came, as through light comes shade,
Cries like an undertone.

Plumed with torn cloud March led the
way
With spear-point keen for thrust,
And eager eyes, and harnessed form swathed grey

With drifts of wind-blown dust.
Round his bruised buckler, in bright letters, lay
   This scroll which toilers trust ; —
   Non sine pulvere.

   Wet as from weltering showers and
      seas,
   April came after him.
He held a cup with saddest imageries
   Engraven, and round the rim,
Worn with woe's lip, I spelt out words like these,
   All sorrow-stained and dim ; —
   Non sine lacrymis.

   These passed like regal spirits crowned,
   Strong March and April fair,
And then a sphere-made music slow unwound
   Its soul upon the air,
And soft as exhalations from the ground
   Or spring-flowers here and there,
   These words rose through the sound :

   " Man needs these two for this world's
      moil,

Earth's drought and dew of spheres,
Grief's freshening rain to lay the dust of toil,
Toil's dust to dry the tears.
To all who rise as wrestlers in life's coil
Time brings with days and years
The wrestler's sand and oil."

O Toil in vain, without surcease!
O Grief no hand may stay!
Think on these words when work or woes increase;
Man made of tears and clay,
Grows to full stature and God's perfect peace,
Non sine pulvere,
Non sine lacrymis.

APOLLO.

(CHANT ROYAL.)

He comes, he comes! Look where yon hill's
    warm crest
    Burns through the breaking cloud, and as a
    key,
Opens the sun-bright portals of the west,
    Where One in glory shines. 'Tis he, 'tis he!
Fairest of Gods where all so fair are found,
Gold-haired and ivory-limbed, and thick around
    Wait Bards august like windless flames aglow,
    While near him, as a wreath of eddying snow,
His thrice-three Sisters dance in circling throng,
    Answering his harp with sweet voice to and
    fro ; —
Paian Apollo, Lord of light and song.

Hark! theirs are sphere-born harmonies heard
    best

By the soul's ear. At their song calm and
   free
The tranced air is lulled in listening rest,
   And Earth is aching with the melody, —
Aching to hear her pent pain half unbound
In thy clear luting, O thou Laurel-Crowned!
   And Night, unmindful of her wonted woe,
   Checks her dun tides in their returning flow,
Lingering amid her stars and listening long,
   Till thy sun-gate soft-shuts with music slow;
Paian Apollo, Lord of light and song!

Whose strain, save thine, assures us, we are blest?
   Not Hermes', nor that harper's of the sea,
Whom the charmed waves once welcomed as their
     guest,
   Nor Orpheus', nor Amphion's minstrelsy,
Nor Pan's reed-murmur, dull bemusing sound,
Born in dark places 'neath or near the ground.
   Such strains hold sway o'er thoughtless lives
     and low.
   But thine unlock all flowerlike souls that blow

In the sky's gardens; thoughts that work no
    wrong;
    Truth, Knowledge, Life's undreamed-of em-
      bryo;
Paian Apollo, Lord of light and song!

Yet oh, how bitter was the Fates' behest,
    Ere thy full prophet-gift was formed in thee!
How in poor neatherd's guise thy life confessed
    That the world's king must first a servant be.
What grief was thine o'er Hyacinth in death-
    swound!
What wandering through the drear North's
    wintry bound!
    What anguish, — with the Love-God for thy
      foe, —
    To love, still doomed the love-bliss to forego!
Ah me! how oft thy sons have fared along
    The same sad path and felt the same heart-
    throe,
Paian Apollo, Lord of light and song!

But see! from out his quiver's burning nest

What flame-fledged arrows fly! Before them
  flee
The Python shapes of dark ill-brooding breast.
  But when thy chosen feel thy dart's decree,
They drop this coil without a pang unwound,
And pass where songs and nectared feasts abound,
  Now could I taste the sleep thy shafts
    bestow,
  Die into life and stay no more below,
But be as thou art, beautiful and strong,
  Fed on the lore which Gods immortal know, —
Paian Apollo, Lord of light and song!

ENVOI.

God of the Lyre! to thee thy poets owe
All kindling sounds that through their king-
  dom go.
Glory to thee, to whom for aye belong
  The World's wide harp and Thought's fire-
    shafted bow, —
Paian Apollo, Lord of light and song!

THE WOODLAND STREAM.

It is not now as it was then,
    Dear Stream, when last I looked on thee ;
Thy world of joy, as mine with men,
    Hath ceased to be.

'Tis past ; and Winter now is come
    To turn to dross thy summer's gold ;
Each hill seems distant ; Earth is dumb ;
    The sun looks old.

I scarcely can believe the moon
    Has filled but thrice since I was here.
King August kept high court that noon,
    When I drew near.

His leafy world with wavelike rush,
    The quick whoop of the whippoorwill
And the slow treble of the thrush
    Were never still.

And, as the breezes went and came,
    The cardinal flowers beside thy brink,
In one long wavering fringe of flame,
    Did shake and shrink.

The joy which Man ne'er understands
    Was thine, thou happy Brook, that day.
How thou didst laugh and clap thy hands
    And bound away!

With that, there broke from bird and tree
    Tumultuous praise, and in their ranks
Those cardinal flowers bowed down to thee
    Along thy banks.

I praised thee too; but soon I sighed:—
    Flow on, dear woodland Stream, flow on;
Laugh while thou mayst; thy summer's pride
    Will soon be gone.

Then with the forest's shattered lute
    Hung silent o'er thy frozen bed,
Thou shalt lie motionless and mute,
    Dead with the dead.

Such bodings of my wayward woe
　　To-day thy waters put to shame ;
Here in their changeless pulse and flow
　　They pass the same.

Some strength is thine which is not ours ;
　　Else, when thy world of joy is gone,
Thou couldst not thus through songless bowers
　　Be flowing on.

Oh, be it mine, when comes the snow
　　And hopes no more are on the wing,
Like thee in feeling still to flow,
　　Like thee to sing.

TRICHORDON.

I met at peep of day
Sadness, twin daughter of divine Unrest,
   In hood and stole of grey.
And Longing, raimented like one distressed.
   With these a Shepherd came
   His eyes and hair like flame,
Fingering a double pipe, Desire by name, —
Desire who leads his pasturing dreams abroad
   Through fields of hope and fear. To whom,
   " My house," I said, " denies ye room ; "
And my heart answered, all unawed,
      " Sigh, sigh no more."

   I wrought of sheltering leaves
A faery house with this sign, "Come not nigh,
   Grief, or thy child that grieves,
Young Dream or tongueless Tear or murmuring
   Sigh,

Or flocks of blithe Desire
Which fare and feed like fire,
Sadness and Longing, to your cells retire.
So shall my spirit rest from strain and strife."
Then, as the dusk which weeps in dew
O'er the dead sun, a drear voice grew, —
O 'twas the voice of Death-in-Life,
    "Love, love no more."

My heart said, "Be it so,
Less love, less care ; no love brings sure relief.
Back to his world I throw
Love's flowers, which fading turn their balms to
    grief."
Forth from my door I spurned
Each love-flower Love had earned,
Turned to my empty house, and, as I turned,
The stars went wailing slow their dying hymn,
And God himself, no more divine,
Burned low on Life's last altar-shrine,
Then sighed to all his worlds death-dim,
    "Live, live no more."

BENEATH HER FEET.

Oh, the rich high harvest night,
    When I kissed and called her mine,
When the barn was lined with light
    And all flowers of bloomy twine.
Twanged the viol, and she came
    In the middle of the floor,
And her light steps flew like flame
    Which the west wind bloweth o'er.
Vain the bow that flashed so fleet,
    Vain the twittering notes it tried,
To the music of her feet
    Sure the fiddle swooned and died.
        I drew near :
And each naked foot that fell
Like a smooth pink-tinted shell
'Neath her ankle's upward swell,
        Chimed as clear

As a faery's wedding bell
       In mine ear.
Then I stooped low as I might, Mary,
    To the ground you made so sweet,
And I whispered soft ; " Step light, Mary,
    For my heart's beneath your feet."

Oh, the dreary New Year's eve,
       When Love came in Love's despair,
Saying, " Where sweet Love would live,
       Sorrow's self must enter there."
For she passed me in the lane,
       Near yon pine, our trysting-place,
With proud step and slow disdain
       In her mute and moon-soft face;
And she held the rich man's arm,
       She, his last doll tricked out new
In the gawds that kept her warm,
       Snow-white plume, silk skirt and shöe.
       I came near :
Each slow scornful step that fell
'Neath her ankle's hidden swell

Rang a slow-paced funeral knell,
     Near, more near ;
As a lost soul's passing bell
     Tolling drear.
Then I stooped low as I might, Mary,
     To your ear, Love's mercy-seat,
Sighing ; "Be not proud ; Step light, Mary,
     This poor heart's beneath your feet."

See, the blush of spring is here,
     Whilst through all my bloodless frame
Autumn spreads its dying year,
     And men know me but by name.
By the sea-sprent abbey-wall
     Grows the sward with April bloom,
Day by day, till death's low call
     Folds it back to give me room.
Soon her eyes shall cease with joy
     In their starry spells to wind him,
Soon he'll toss his broken toy
     In the dust of days behind him.
        Then if near

Where I sleep, she seeks the sod,
With her foot once more unshod,
Hair unbound and blown abroad,
  And her tear
Falls like fire which comes from God, —
  Hear me, hear ;
Bending low before you part, Mary,
  Let my dust these words repeat ;
" O step light ; for this poor heart, Mary,
  Still is yours beneath your feet."

KISSES AND TEARS.

" Take this, a kiss "— Such words fell on mine ear,
 As through the green gloom of a lawny glade,
 For Love's high feast arrayed
In blood-red raiment, Love himself drew near.
With motion, voice and look divinely blent,
Like one sweet sound of many an instrument,
 He came and breathed on me, then smiled and
  drew
From a small casket stored with balmy bliss
 Such drops of honey-dew,
 As his mouth, beelike, sips
 From the warm, flower-soft lips
Of all who ever kissed beneath the moon ; —
 Saying as he gave the boon,
  " Take this, a kiss."

" Drink here, a tear : Love needs the seasoning
 brine."
 Clad in grey stole with pansies dark inwrought,

Feeding his speechless thought,
Love stood and called me to his wayside shrine,
Where, grey with grief, many a late-answered
        Prayer
Knelt on her knee-worn sanctuary stair,
        While in a cup, with rosemary wreathed and
        rue,
He, priestlike, to their lips and mine brought near
        The sacramental dew,
        Drawn from the darkling deep
        Into which angels weep.
Then sighing, " Take this, my second sacrament,"
        He murmured, as he went,
                " Drink here, a tear."

" Kisses and tears !   What Love gives, Love must
        keep."
        Love spake and came to Life's death-darkened
        house,
        Black-robed, and round his brows
Drooped lotus-flowers and poppies drenched in
        sleep.

"Give me an alms," he cried, "our house is poor,
And she thou lov'st now dwells within our door.

 'Twas I who brought her, I who took her
  hence,
Sealing her thine twice for Time's deathless years
 In my twin sacraments."
 Life's bankrupt, yet Love's heir,
 I knelt in darkness there,
And saying, "Take all I have for drink or meat,"
 Rained on Love's naked feet
  Kisses and tears.

THE IMPOSSIBLE SHE.

Whoe'er she be,
That not impossible She,
That shall command my heart and me.

— *Crashaw.*

Far away hangs an apple that ripens on high,
The latest-born child of old sun-blind July,
Till the summer's warm kiss as he wooes overhead
Turns its sour heart to sweetness, its wan cheek to
red.
But it is not for you, and it is not for me,
Nay, it is not for any who here may be;
For its dawning red sweetness,
That rounds to completeness,
Grows moist for the lips that we never may
see.

There's a white rose leaf-cloistered in heavy noon-
hush,
And no eyes but the stars tempt its pale face to
blush,

In that wilderness garden where, shut from day's
beam,

Fall its fragrant white leaves light as steps of a
dream.

But it is not for you, and it is not for me,

Nay, it is not for any who here may be ;

For it sleeps and then wakes

In dew-scented snow-flakes,

As a star for the dusk hair we never may see.

In a green golden valley there grows an elf-girl,

And her lip is red-ripe, and her soul, one rich pearl,

Yields once to one diver a treasure unpriced

As the wine of the Gods or the wine-blood of
Christ.

But she is not for you, and she is not for me,

Nay, she is not for any who here may be ;

For her breast like a moon

Through the rosed air of June

Grows round for his hand whom we never
may see.

WHEN LOVE GROWS OLD.

Now say what thing remains
  When the smiles fly ;
    When the lips keep
    A stillness deep
    As death or sleep,
  And the smiles fly ;
Now say what thing remains
  When the smiles fly.

One thing remains for thee ;
  From grief's moist sphere,
    Without thy call
    Ripe fruit will fall,
    On thee, the thrall
  Of Love's last fear ;
One thing remains for thee, —
  There comes the tear.

Now say what thing remains
  When the tears pass ;
    When from grief sown
    New Love upgrown
    Leads forth his own,
  And the tears pass ;
Now say what thing remains
  When the tears pass.

One thing remains for thee
  Of perfect bliss ;
    Without thy call
    Sweet dew will fall,
    To lift Love's thrall
  From Death's abyss ;
One thing remains for thee,
  There comes the kiss.

Now say what thing remains
  When kisses die ;
    When Love's bee slips
    Off the pressed lips
    And no more sips,

And kisses die ;
Now say what thing remains
When kisses die.

One thing remains for thee ;
There comes a Dove
Without thy call,
And She lets fall
On thee, Heaven's thrall,
The fruits thereof ;
One thing remains for thee,
And that is Love.

Now say what thing remains
When Love grows old ;
When the smiles fly,
When the tears dry
When kisses die,
And Love grows old ;
Now say what thing remains
When Love grows old.

One thing remains for thee
Or soon or late ;

Without thy call
Strange fruit will fall
On thee, the thrall
Of loveless fate ;
One thing remains for thee,
And that — is Hate.

TOMORROW.

Let us eat and drink, for tomorrow —
    We die.
Let us eat and drink.   Wherefore borrow
   From griefs that will never come nigh?
   Spread the feast, pour the wine,
   Wreathe the brows with rose-twine,
Woo the harp into pulses of passion divine.
   Remember how soon
   The belfry's dull rune
Shall summon us hence from our comrades boon.
   Then deaf to their cry,
Unheeding the tears of this sorrow,
   How low we shall lie!
Then, eat and drink, for tomorrow —
    We die.

Let us love and laugh, for tomorrow —
    We die.
Let us love and laugh.   Why should Sorrow

Kill Feeling so soon with a sigh?
Laugh and love, love and laugh.
Who mourns lives but half.
Life's joy is the grain, its grief is the chaff.
Rejoice while we may,
For December's dark day
Swift spurs with his scythe our first fancies away,
And the tear-clouds on high
From seas of new anguish will borrow
To darken thine eye.
Then love and laugh, for tomorrow —
We die.

Let us clasp and kiss, for tomorrow —
We die.
Let us clasp and kiss. How can Sorrow
Endure, while sweet Love stands by?
Why live we so far,
When passion's white star
Draws close these two hearts that confederate are?
Let our souls mix and flow
And our quick kisses go,

While these breasts are like fire-buds, these brows
    are of snow.
    Pluck the sweets that are nigh.
Life's our own, not a treasure we borrow
    From Gods in the sky.
Then, clasp and kiss, for tomorrow —
    We die.

AMERICA'S ANSWER.

1861 — 1885.

Now twice twelve years ago,
When we, through fields of woe,
Weeping went forth to sow
    Our blood's red seed,
We cried to the old-world land ;
" These fresh wounds crave your hand,
Help us to balm and band
    In our sore need."

Then back their message ran ;
" Renounce your cloud-born plan,
Deeming that man with man
    Can live thus free :
Unbind the lictor's rod,
Teach old Disdain to nod,
Throne Custom for your god
    And — live as We."

Those twice twelve years are gone
War's harvest work is done,
All our stars sing as one
    From sea to sea :
While far across the main,
Their skies grow black with rain,
Where the old world cries in pain,
    " Your help need We."

Back flies our answering word ;
" Free your soil, sheathe your sword,
Live ye in love's accord,
    As men ; be free ;
Be one ; — till Peace creates,
High above gods and fates,
A World's United States,
    And— Live as We."

VIVE VALEQUE.

To Robert Dwyer Joyce.

[In the year 1883, Boston lost, within six weeks, two distinguished artistic workmen. On the 21st of July died Martin
Milmore, the sculptor of the Soldiers' Monument and the
Sphinx in Mount Auburn. On the 2d of September, sailed
for Ireland, in shattered health, Robert Dwyer Joyce, Poet
and Physician, the author of "Deirdre" and "Blanid."]

O saddest of all the sea's daughters, Ierne, dear
    mother isle,

Take home to thy sweet, still waters thy son whom
    we lend thee awhile.

Twenty years has he poured out his song, epic
    echoes heard in our street,

Twenty years have the sick been made strong as
    they heard the sound of his feet.

For few there be in his lands whom Apollo deigns
    to choose,

On whose heads to lay both hands in medicine-gift
    and the muse.

Double-grieved because double-gifted now take him
    and make strong again

The heart long-winnowed and sifted on the thresh-
ing-floor of pain.

Saving others, he saved not himself, like a ship-
master staunch and brave,

Whose men leave the surge-beaten shelf, while he
sinks alone in the wave.

The child in the night cries "mother," and the
mother straight brings peace ;

Ierne, be kind to our brother; speak thou, and
his plague shall cease.

Thou gavest him once, as revealer, song-breath and
the starry scroll,

Give him now, as the heart's best healer, life-breath
and balms for the soul.

O saddest of all the sad islands, green-girt by thy
mother the sea,

Fold warm, and feed with thy silence the child
whom we send to thee.

Two children thou gavest our city, to stand in the
stress and strife,

And touch us to holier pity through shapes of the
deathless life ;
One caught in the mountain granite, the other in
marble of song,
Those shadows that fall on our planet from the
worlds of the Fair and the Strong ;
Of those thy two sons thou gavest, one is, but the
younger is not ;
For with all men, even the bravest, strength wanes,
when the noons wax hot.
The wine of his life half tasted, the work of his
life half done,
He sank through earth-wounds that wasted, heart-
sore and sick of the sun,
The scabbard fell from the sabre, the soul dropped
its time-worn vest,
Then we said, Let this land of his labor be always
the land of his rest,
And always the bronze and the stone that grew
soft to his touch as flame,
Shaped for others, shall now be his own, new-raised
and emblazed with his name,

And the glimmering shaft that catches the sun's
last kiss on his head,*
And the Sphinx that overwatches the unmurmur-
ing streets of the dead,
Shall call to life's tide where it dashes, and speak
of him we deplore,
Till the sun burns down to ashes, and the moon
cries, I rise no more.

Who shall cancel that which is sealed? Who shall
close what the Fates have cleft?
Two men were at work in one field; one is taken,
the other left;
He is left in life's mid meadows, nor yet have the
days begun,
When the hand from the valley of shadows draws
down from the light of the sun;
He lives, and looks round with dread, as a strength-
less reaper who grieves,
When the last low moon rises red on his rich half
harvested sheaves.

* The Soldiers' Monument on Boston Common and the
Sphinx at Mount Auburn.

Hast not thou, Ierne, a blossom that scared the
    snake from thy soil,

That shall slay the snake in the bosom and wither
    its deadly coil ?

Yea, thou hast what we fain would inherit, though
    kings in these isles of the blest,

Thou hast for the world-worn spirit some simples
    unfound in the West.

Here the field flows with milk and honey, the river
    with spoil divine,

Here the clear air is warm with sunny gold cups
    of invisible wine,

Self-trust and Toil are defiant, and Freedom is
    mightier than these,

And Wealth spreads his couch, like a giant, silk-
    smooth for the sides of Ease,

And gilds man and man with his million, and fast
    as he flies through the heat,

White cabin and purple pavilion are stirred with the
    storm of feet.

But what soil, thou Eden of islands, can match thy
    red and white store,

The roses of health on thy highlands, the lilies of
    love on thy shore?
What land lies emerald-valleyed, inlaid with lakelet
    and lawn,
Where the spirit is swifter rallied, reclothed as
    with lights of the dawn?
Or where comes with starrier splendor the touch
    of a light-breathing fan,
To scatter the chaff, and make tender and affluent
    the spirit of man?
There a courtier is found in the cot, and a prince
    in the poor man's shed,
With a soul sorrow-born, love-begot, rocked and
    cradled in thoughts of the dead,
A soul like a wind-harp that plays all tones of
    laughter and tears,
Now burns, now in dying delays woos us back
    through its dream of the years.
There the neediest spreads you the last of his earth
    apples dug from the ground,
And the salt of his wit turns the fast to a feast
    where dainties abound, —

Smile and tear and manna-dropt speech freely
    shed on the least word he saith,
And high-soaring thought beyond reach and the
    love of his land to the death.

Sweetest isle of old white-haired Ocean, breathe
    new in this child of thy love
A spirit whose musical motion is light as the wings
    of a dove,
While hence, from palace and purlieu, our messen-
    ger-thoughts on the breeze
Shall reach him through cry of curlew and call of
    sundering seas,
Where perchance, in the shore-wind's breathing,
    he looks from some headland height,
His westward-bound thoughts bequeathing to the
    sun ere he sinks in night,
Or haply mid stones of the olden and perilous places
    of fear,
He rears a new song-palace, golden with dreams of
    meadow and mere,

Mab's realm, the swart Connaught Queen, faery
  bugles blown thro' the sky,
Magic shores, which once to have seen is to live
  and never die ;
Where Benbulben, lonely and solemn, looks forth
  tow'rd dark Donegal,
O'er the endless Atlantic column that foams round
  Sliev League's rock-wall,
Down whose cliff the Gods drave their share and
  its face with long furrows ploughed,
When they planted as king of the air, crag-throned
  and ermined with cloud,
The far-sighted, sun-gazing eagle to scream to the
  deep his decree,
Low-boomed in organ-tones regal and vassal voices
  of sea.

O saddest of all the sea's daughters, Ierne, sweet
  mother isle,
Say, how canst thou heal at thy waters the son
  whom we lend thee awhile ?

When the gathering cries implore thee to help and
to heal thy kind,
When thy dying are strewn before thee, thy living
ones crouch behind,
When about thee thy perishing children cling, crying, "Thou only art fair,
We have seen through Life's maze bewildering how
the earth-gods never spare:"
And the wolves blood-ripe with slaughter gnar at
thee with fangs of steel ;
Thou, Emerald Star of the water, hast many children to heal.
Yet heal him, Ierne, dear mother, thy days with
his days shall increase,
At the song of this Delphic brother, nigh half of
thy pangs shall cease.

Nor art thou, sweet friend, in a far land, — all
places are near on the globe,
Our greeting wear for thy garland, our love for thy
festival robe,

While we keep through glory and gloom two altar-
candles for thee,
Thy "Blanid" of deathless doom, and thy dead
but undying "Deirdrè."
And may He who builds in his patience the houses
which death reveals,
Round whom the far constellations are dust from
his chariot-wheels,
Who showers his coin without scorning, each day
as he issues it bright,
The sun as his gold in the morning, the stars as his
silver at night,
The love which feedeth the sparrow and watcheth
the little leaf,
Which guideth the death-laden arrow and counteth
each grain of grief,
Change thy life-chant from its minor and spread
thy spirit serene,
As gold before the refiner whose face is reflected
therein.

SONNET.

James Abram Garfield, September 19th, 1881.

Lo ! as a pure white statue wrought with care
　By some strong hand that moulds with tear and
　　sigh
　Beauty more beautiful than things that die,
And straight 'tis veiled ; and whilst all men repair
To see this wonder in the workshop, there !
　Behold, it gleams unveiled to curious eye,
　Far-seen, high-placed in Art's pale gallery,
Where all stand mute before a work so fair :
So he, our man of men, in vision stands,
　With Pain and Patience crowned imperial ;
　Death's veil has dropped ; far from this house of
　　woe
He hears one love-chant out of many lands,
　Whilst from his mystic morn-height he lets fall
　His shadow o'er these hearts that bleed below.

FRYEBURG — 1882.

No vale with purer peace the spirit fills
    Than thine, Fryeburg the fair, Fryeburg the free.
    Dear are thy men and maidens unto me ;
Holy the smokeless altars of thy hills ;
    Sacred thy wide, moist meadows, where the morn
    Delays for very love ; divinely born
Those drooping tresses of thy feathery elms,
    That lisp of cool delight through dreams of noon ;
    Gentle thy Saco's tides, that creep and croon,
Lapsing and lingering through hushed forest-
    realms,
    Which love the song-bird's boon.

But neither vale nor hill nor field nor tree
    Nor stream nor forest had this day been ours,
    Nor would sweet English speech in Fryeburg's
    bowers
This night be heard across her lake and lea, —
    Our seamless flag had been in pieces riven,

Nor had we been, beneath its blue, starred
   heaven,
A nation one and indivisible, —
   Had not two spirits come to range and reign
   Here over sand-girt Saco's green domain,
The one with sword, th' other with prophet-spell, —
   Webster and Chamberlain.

Two crowns of glory clasp thy calm, chaste brow.
   O ye strong hills, bear witness to my verse,
   Thou " Maledotto," mountain of the curse,*
Chocorua, blasted by thy chief, and thou,
   Kearsarge, slope-shouldered monarch of this
      vale,
   Who gav'st thy conquering name to that swift
      sail
Which caught in Gallic seas the rebel bark,
   And downward drove the *Alabama's* pride
   To deep sea-sleep in Cherbourg's ravening tide,

---

* Mt. Maledotto, the Chocorua of the Pyrenees, is entirely
destitute of vegetation, the supposed result of a malediction
like that pronounced by the Indian chieftain.

What time faint Commerce watched a nation's ark
    Sinking with shattered side.

Speak, ye historian pine-woods, where ye stand,
    And thou bald scalp, like the bald crown of
        time,*
    Lifted above thy sylvan sea sublime,
And ye still shores, reaches of golden sand,
    Linked like a necklace round your Lovell's lake,
    Speak, for ye saw how, when the morning brake,
Brave Chamberlain, and men like Chamberlain,
    Like lions turned, where round them in fell scorn
    Leaped from their lairs a thousand flushed with
        morn,
And fought, death-loving, grand in life's disdain,
    Till eve's first star was born.

Then fell the peerless, fearless, cheerless chief,
    Paugus, between this water and that wood,
    Staining the yellow strand with Indian blood,
Death-struck by Chamberlain ; and straight in grief

---

* Equestrian fancy calls the scalp-like rock overhanging
" Jockey Cap."

The Indian vanished, and the English came,
And laid on this lone mere their Lovell's name,
Lovell who led them: thus the northern land
From Kearsarge to Katahdin, and the State
Named from the Pine, lay open as a gate
For Saxon steps to reach St. Lawrence strand,
Clear of wild war's debate.

A century, half a hundred years, and seven,
Each like a pilgrim from eternity
With sandals of soft silence creeping by,
Have paced thy streets, and hied them home to
heaven,
Sweet Fryeburg, since thy Lovell's battle-day
Wove the pine-wreath which welcomes no decay;
But grandsire Time, who crowns men with both
hands,
Giving to him that hath, decreed that thou,
Ere fourscore years, shouldst bind about thy
brow
A second wreath, culled from thy meadow-lands
And the elm's peaceful bough.

Then Judgment rose on swift, storm-shadowed
    wings,*

And pitying Man, heart-sick with vain desire,

Sent him new Gods, mist-robed and crowned
    with fire,

To trace with flame-like hands the doom of kings.

Through the worn world, like throb of morning
    drum,

Pealed the fierce shout, — the new Gods' reign is
    come ;

And new-risen stars, ablaze round Man's new bride,

Came down to sing at Freedom's marriage feast

When through the listening lands of West and
    East,

A Daniel rose for judgment on each side

Where the Atlantic ceased.

---

* " A Daniel come to judgment, yea, a Daniel." Two young
champions of popular freedom, each bearing this name, arose
almost in the same hour on either side of the Atlantic. In 1800,
while the bells of St. Patrick's Cathedral were ringing triumph-
antly over the downfall of the old Irish Parliament, young
Daniel O'Connell rose in the Corn Exchange, Dublin, and
delivered his maiden speech. In 1802 young Daniel Webster
spoke for the first time, and in the spirit of the same political
principles.

Twenty rich summers glowed along his veins
  When from New Hampshire's high-born hills a
    youth
  Came down, a seeker and a sayer of sooth,
To stand beneath these elms, and shake the reins
  That steer the heart of boyhood's fiery prime.
  They called him Daniel Webster, and the chime
Measured the sliding hours with smooth, slow
    stroke,
  While he sat registering the deed, and wrought
  As though the wide world watched him : swift
    in thought,
But slow in speech ; yet once, when once he spoke,
  Then an archangel taught.

'Twas Magna Charta's morning in July,
  When, in that temple reared of old to Truth,
  He rose, in the bronze bloom of blood-bright
    youth,
To speak, what he re-spake when death was nigh.*
  Strongly he stood, Olympian-framed, with front

* Webster, in his last speech in the Senate, repeated the
peroration of his Fryeburg oration; an example of the law
under which many other supreme artists have been led to
work over and enlarge the lines of their life's first efforts.

Like some carved crag where sleeps the light-
ning's brunt;
Black, thunderous brows, and thunderous deep-
toned speech
Like Pericles, of whom the people said,
That, when he spake, it thundered; round him
spread
The calm of summer nights when the stars teach
In silence overhead.

Lift up thy head, behold thy citizen,
O Fryeburg! From thy cloistered shades
came he, —
Who came like many more who come from
thee, —
To teach the cities how the hills make men.
Guard thy unabdicated pastoral throne,
God-kept within thy God-made mountain zone, —
Of Truth, of Love, of Peace, the worshipper;
Keep fresh thy double garland, and hand down
This my last leaf woven in thy Webster's crown,
And leave lean Envy's loathed, unkennelled cur
To bark at his renown.

A NEW ENGLAND WINTER SONG.

FOREFATHERS' DAY, DECEMBER 22.

Who cradled thee on the rock, my boy,
  Far, far from the sun-warm South?
Who woke thee with shout and shock, my boy,
  And spray for a kiss on thy mouth,
As the low, sad shores grew dim with rain
And the grey sea moaned its infinite pain
To grey grass and pale sands, thy sole domain?
  Who cradled thee on the rock?

I brought thee into the wilderness,
  When thou didst cry to me,
And I gave thee there in thy sore distress
  The rock and the cloud and the sea;
With baptismal waves thy limbs were wet,
And the ragged cloud was thy coverlet, —
Thus saith the Lord God: Dost thou forget?
  I cradled thee on the rock.

Who shadowed thee with the cloud, my boy;
   And the stars forgat to shine,
And the sun lay as dead in his shroud, my boy,
   And thy tears were to thee for wine?
Who took from thee every pleasant thing,
Sweet sounds that are drawn from stop and string,
Day's dream and the night's glad banqueting?
   Who shadowed thee with the cloud?

I broke thy slumber with clarion storms,
   I called like a midnight bell,
Till thou saw'st thro' the dark the spirit-forms,
   Heaven's glow and the glare of hell;
And then, that thou mightest know God's grace
And drink his love-wine and see his face,
I drew thee into my secret place, —
   I shadowed thee with the cloud.

Who fenced thee round with the sea, my boy,
   And locked its gates amain?
Who, to set thy fathers free, my boy,
   Burst the bars of the deep in twain,

And led them by ways they knew not of,
When the black storm spread its wings above
And thundered, My God is Law, not Love !
  Who fenced thee round with the sea ?

I set thee beyond where the great sea ran,
  I made thee to dwell apart,
For in the divisions of man from man
  Come the mighty searchings of heart ;
I, the Lord, who moved on the waters old,
Who sought for a heart like the sea's heart, —
    bold,
Unchartered, chainless, and myriad-souled —
  I fenced thee round with the sea.

ODE TO GENERAL PORFIRIO DIAZ.*

EX-PRESIDENT OF THE UNITED STATES OF MEXICO.

I.

Open thy storm-dark doors, dear Northern Land,
  Star-diademed, pale Priestess of the free,
  Walled round by wind and water and that grey
    sea
Whose morning psalm salutes his Pilgrims' strand,
  O thou to whom all great things thought and
    done
Are dear, all fights for Freedom lost or won,
  Queen of the earth's free states,
  Open to him thy gates,
This champion of the children of the Sun ;
  To him who with his king-destroying rod
  Wiped the last king-curse from the southern
    sod

* Read at the banquet in Boston, April 11th, 1883.

Bring the loud welcome which the freeman
   brings,
When his full harp is struck thro' all its strings
With music born of God.

II.

He comes a hero to a heroes' home,
   New England's hills, peal forth your thrice All
   Hail,
   Far as the Gulf, till every seaward sail
Bends low to hear, and Orizaba's dome
   Heaves his flame-hearted breast of barren brown
   And breaks the frosts that bind his helmet-
   crown,
   To see his realm re-born,
   Which late the old worlds could scorn,
Now nearer to life's flowering marge of morn ;
   To see his country's chief and chosen thereof
   In war and peace its eagle and its dove,
Called here to reap the far fruits of past pain
And bear New England's blessing to New Spain
   With the strong Northman's love.

III.

The Pine-tree waves her peace-pledge to the Palm,
  Sending sweet grace and greeting, not as they
  Who greet and give not.   For in time's past day,
Ere thy quick South roused from their summer-
      calm
  Her baby Hopes adream on wings warm-furled,
  Our seedplot for all gardens of the world
    Nursed through its bud and birth
    One tree, till the whole earth
  Owned its circumferent leaves and giant girth;
    Whence winnowed by the northwind's wings
      of power
  A fire-seed smote thy soil, and lo! a bower,
A blossom-blaze, a Maytime glorious.
O gardener, what is this thou bringest us?
  Our freedom's far-sown flower.

IV.

O Tree of Liberty, thou Tree of Life,
  Without thee what were all the golden South?
  The Cid's rich song from ripe Castilian mouth;

The eyes' black velvet of each gay girl-wife ;
  The scarlet nopal, jasmine's earth-born star ;
  The low bird-language of the light guitar
    Wooed by love's wandering hand ;
    And teocalli grand,
  With scroll and sculptured face of mild command;
    Querêtaro's wave-worn arches, one long mile
    Of marching giants ; Viga's floating isle ;
  Cholula's hill-shrine of the all-worshipped Sun ;
  Huge cypress shade ; all Aztec spoils in one,
    Without thee were most vile.

V.

Look whither Nature leads thee, soldier-priest ;
  Not South to soil war-scourged and thunder-
    scarred,
  Not West where friendship fails thee ocean-
    barred,
Not to the palsied, mad, monarchic East,
  Dazzling with sunlike gems of gay romance
  And backward gaze fixed in tradition's trance,
    Who sent across the main

The monkish spawn of Spain,
And Austria's yellow plague and black Bazaine,
   To lash thy land with battle's gory shower
   And cage thee in Puebla's dungeon-tower,
Whence rushed thy eagle spirit new-fledged,
      and burst
The death-folds of the serpent crowned and
      cursed,
   When hell lost half her power.

VI.

The strongest Gods dwell ever in the North,
   In labor's land and sorrow's; but at length
   Labor and sorrow bring the perfect strength.
See, from Ezekiel's northern hills leaps forth
   The car of crystal floor and sapphire throne,
   In amber-colored light and rainbow zone,
      On self-moved beryl wheels,
      Through fire-mist that reveals
Man, its great charioteer, aloft, alone,
      Where round him float three mystic shapes
         divine,

Cloven foot of steer, and starred wing aquiline,
And lion's regal mane ready to rise,
Like slumbering Law, on all its enemies,
In strength, O guest, like thine.

VII.

So to thy home sweeps down unconquerable
Our iron chariot of the prophet's dream,
Fire-fledged and clothed in cloud and wreathed
with steam,
Flashed like a poet's thought through all — cleft
hill,
Rent rock and rolling flood and fiery sand,
Laden with Life's humanities, not the brand
Of widow-making war,
To blast thy fields afar,
Like burnings of the intolerable star.
So flies the thunder-bearing steed of flame
Waking each southern silence with *his* name,*
King of his kinsman round the stormy cape,

* Thomas Nickerson, Esq., president of the Mexican Central Railroad.

Whose heart, head, hand to purpose, plan and
    shape,
Win him a conquerer's fame.

VIII.

Thee, latest-born, self-liberated State,
    Earth, heaven and thy two Oceans wait to bless.
    Our blessing also take, with love not less,
As of thy sister ever inseparate,
    And take thy place in the immemorial line
    Of those that soared and sang with hopes
        like thine,
      And with voice clear, and strong,
      And piercing sweet, prolong
The choral thunders of their mighty song,
    Till earth's new Man, touched by the spirit
        breeze,
    Shall wake to morn's memnonian melodies,
Bright as when Daybreak from his rosy home
Stains with his blood-red life the furrowed foam
    Of sunward-surging seas.

ZEUS AND EUROPA.

AN IDYL.

[FROM THE GREEK OF MOSCHUS — B. C. 300 — 200.]

Once to Europa came a vision sweet
From Venus, at that hour 'twixt dark and dawn
When honeyed Sleep brooding o'er calm-shut eyes
Unchains the limbs and seals the lids of man,
What time true Dreams fare forth in pasturing
    flocks.

High in her palace-chamber, as she slept,
Europa, child of Phœnix, virgin pure,
Her seemed that Asia and its adverse shore
Rose, like two rival women, and claimed her hand.
One wore a stranger's garb, the other seemed
Of her own land, who clung to her and cried :
" This child I bore and nursed her for mine own."
But she, that other, haled her thence perforce,
A willing prize as thus she heard her speak :
" High Zeus, Europa, hath foredoomed thee mine."

Up from her couch the maid in terror sprang
With beating heart, so real was the dream,
And long she sat in wondering trance, and still
Before her waking eyes those women came.
At last she raised her trembling voice, and said :
"What God in heaven hath sent these phantoms
forth ?
What bode these dreams that hovering o'er my bed
Chase the sweet sleep from this my cloistered
bower ?
And who that stranger whom in dreams I saw ?
How my heart yearned for her, and kindly, too,
She greeted me, and looked a mother's love.
Blest Gods, with happy issues crown my dream."

Then rising sought she those companions dear,
Her peers in age, loved of her heart, high-born,
Her mates, whene'er she decked her for the dance,
Or bathed her bright form in the seaward stream,
Or culled the fragrant lilies on the lea.
And straight she found them, each with basket,
bound

In quest of flowers, and to the leas they fared
Hard by the sea, the haunts they loved so well,
Sweet with the bloom of rose and dash of waves.
Now fair Europa's basket was of gold,
A miracle of art, Hephœstus' work,
Which he to Libya gave on that high day
When first she graced the Earth-Shaker's bridal
    bed :
She to fair Telephassa passed it down,
As near of kin, and she on her child unwed,
Europa, next bestowed the priceless gift.
Wherein was many a rich and rare device ;
There shone Inachian Io wrought in gold.
In heifer-shape, waiting her woman's form ;
With restless feet she pawed the bitter brine,
Like one who swims ; the sea was blue inwrought ;
High on a cloven headland groups of men
With wonder saw a heifer roam the sea.
And there stood Zeus, and stroked with hand divine
His hornèd care, till by Nile's sevenfold flood
The heifer took the woman's shape once more.
In silver ran the Nile, the cow was bronze,

The god was gold, and round the basket's rim
Was Hermes quaintly carved, and there, out-
    stretched
Beside him, Argus with his sleepless eyes,
While from his crimson blood uprose a bird
Proud in its plumage gay with many flowers,
Whose train outspread, like to some full-winged
    ship,
O'erlaid the basket's lips with feathers bright ;
Such was the heirloom in Europa's hand.

Into the blooming leas the maidens came
And each with glad heart culled some favorite
    flower,
Here the narcissus, there the hyacinth,
The violet, and the creeping thyme, till the earth
Lay thick-strewn with the falling blooms of spring :
Some ran to pluck the crocus' yellow locks,
But in their midst the princess proudly shone,
Gathering the glories of the crimson rose,
As mid her Graces shines the Foam-born Queen.
But she not long might feast her heart on flowers,

Nor long might keep her maiden zone unbound.
For soon as Zeus beheld her, was he snared,
Soul-smitten by a love-dart unforeseen
From her, sole conqueress e'en of Zeus himself.
But to escape his Hera's jealous wrath
And win with stealth the maiden's untried heart,
He veiled his Godhead and became a bull;
Not such as those that feed in earthly stalls
Or draw the share, ploughing the furrowed field,
Or crop the grass or hale the loaded wain.
His bulk was clothed in hide of golden hue,
Between his brows a snow-white circle gleamed,
And soft desire flashed from those pale blue eyes,
O'er which, like circlets of the crescent moon,
In even balance rose the branching horns.

He came into the lea ; no fear possessed
Those maidens, but a love to come and touch
The beauteous bull, who sweeter than the breath
Of meadow shed immortal odors round.
Now before chaste Europa's feet he stood,

And licked her neck, and soothed her with his
    spells.
She too caressed him, and with gentle hand
Wiped the thick foam away, and kissed the bull,
Then softly lowed he that ye fain had said
Ye heard the clear sweet sound of Phrygian flutes.
Low-stooping, he presented his broad back,
Whereat her rich-haired maidens she bespake :
" Come on, my playmates, let us mount this bull,
And seat ourselves for sport ; he will upbear
Like a stout ship, the burthen of us all.
How mild he looks, and gentle, how unlike
All creatures of his sort ; yea, mind he has
Right good, and lacks but speech to be a man."

She said, and smiling, sat her on his back,
The rest were following, but he started up,
His prize now won, and bore her to the deep.
Europa turned, and called and called again
To her dear mates, and stretched out helpless
    hands.
But from the sea-marge, dolphin-like he flew

Athwart the waves with cloven foot unwet.
Before his coming all the sea grew calm,
And huge things gambolled round the feet of Zeus.
Up through the swell the dolphin flounced in glee ;
The Nereids peeped above the brine, and came
All charioted on the backs of sea-born shapes ;
The Earth-Shaker rose, and sent his deep sea-
   voice
Abroad, and laid each wave, and led the way
For his own brother ; all about him trooped
The Tritons, trumpeters of the flowing deep,
Who blew from wreathed shells a bridal strain.

But seated on the bull-formed back of Zeus
Europa went, one hand held fast a horn,
The other updrew her garment's purple fold,
Lest the salt foam should wet its loosening train.
Her swelling vest orbed out in arching folds
A bellying sail to waft her on her way.
Far from her native land when now no more
She saw its wave-washed coast, its climbing hills,
Round her with fearful glance she looked, and said:

"Whither dost thou bear me, Bull-God? Who
    art thou
That with unwonted foot canst traverse thus
The sea, undaunted? Seas are ploughed by ships,
Not steers, which always shun the salt-sea deep?
What food, what sweet drink drawest thou from
    the brine?
Nor dolphins tread the land, nor steers the sea,
But thou o'er sea and land unterrified
With each high-lifted hoof oarest thy way.
Nay, soon perhaps above yon light blue sky
Thou next wilt soar as wingèd bird in flight.
Ah! woe is me, most wretched! Woe is me,
That left my father's home, following this bull,
A lonely wanderer bound for lands unknown!
But, O thou Shaker of the seas and shores,
In mercy come, thee dimly I descry
Smoothing the perilous path whereon I go, —
Not without God I roam this watery waste."

And answer made the Bull of spreading horns,
" Courage, dear maid, fear not the swelling tide.

Know, I am Zeus.   What if this visible mould
Be bull, I can assume what shape I will —
My love of thee hath drawn me in this form
To measure out great spaces of salt sea.
Yonder is Crete, that shall receive thee soon,
My cradle once, and now thy bridal bower.
Yea, sired by me, thy sons shall glorious rise
To stretch the sceptre-staff across the world."

No sooner said than done.   Crete rose in view,
And Zeus resumed his godlike shape once more.
The Hours adorned their bed.   He loosed her
    zone,
And she, a maiden once, became a bride ;
A matron next, and mother of his babes.

THE IDYL OF THE SPRING.

FROM THE GREEK OF BION (B. C. 280).

[Wherein Kléodêmus, a countryman, enquireth of Myrson, which season pleaseth him most; whereunto Myrson, who is yᵉ older and eke yᵉ godlier swain, maketh answer and addeth his reasons therefor.]

KLEODÊMUS.

Myrson, which to thee is sweetest of the seasons
    of the year?
Spring; full autumn; winter; summer;— whose
    loved presence comes most dear?
Summer? when each task is ended, and our toil
    and moil is o'er;
Or lush autumn? when men lack not through the
    fullness of her store;
Or cold winter? when they work not, for 'tis then
    that drowsed and warm
One and all yield up their senses to the fireside's
    listless charm;
Or hath springtide, with her beauty, greater power
    to soothe and please?
Say whilst leisure courts our converse, which dost
    thou prefer of these?

MYRSON.

That we mortals should give sentence on God's
    works is most unmeet,
For these seasons all are sacred, and whate'er he
    makes is sweet,
Yet to please thee, Kleodêmus, I will say which
    suits me best.
Summer, I would ne'er desire thee, with thy swel-
    tering suns oppressed,
Mellow autumn, thee I choose not, for thy ripe
    fruits bring disease.
Cruel winter, how I dread thee and thy snows and
    skies that freeze,
But O spring, thrice loved and longed for, be thou
    with me all the year,
Then shall neither frost nor burthen of the burn-
    ing heat be near.
In the spring the earth, o'erteeming, bears all
    sweet things blooming bright,
And, like gifts in equal measure, falls the dark and
    dawns the light.

RECENT TRAVEL, ETC.

Vigilante Days and Ways: The Pioneers of
the Rockies. By the Hon. N. P. LANGFORD. With portraits and illustrations. 2 vols., 8vo, cloth, 911 pages, $6.00; half morocco, $10.00; full morocco, $12.50.

Remarkable for facts and for being one of the most stirringly written accounts of an otherwise unknown period of American history ever made by a Western author. It throws new light upon the section of the country of which it treats, and upon a class of men of heroic mould but humble origin, whose names now stand high in the New Great West.

Glimpses of Norseland. By HETTA M. HER-
VEY. Illustrated. 1 vol., 16mo, cloth, gilt top, $1.25.

The experiences of a bright American girl among the Scandinavians: crisp and suggestive; showing what to do, what to see, and what not to do.

Bermuda Guide: A description of everything
on and about the Bermuda Islands, concerning which the visitor or resident may desire information, including their history, inhabitants, climate, agriculture, geology, government, military and naval establishments. By JAMES H. STARK, with Maps, Engravings and 16 Photoprints. 1 vol., 12mo, cloth, 157 pages, $2.00.

Bahama Islands: History and guide to the Ba-
hama Islands. By J. H. STARK. With many illustrations. A companion to Bermuda Guide, 12mo, $2.00.

Boating Trips on New England Rivers. By
HENRY PARKER FELLOWS. Illustrated. Square 12mo, cloth, $1.25.

This capital book, the only American work so far upon its subject, was warmly commended by the late John Boyle O'Reilly, who saw in it the beginning of an interest in our American rivers, which he, one of the most enthusiastic of boatmen, did so much to encourage and foster.

Mailed, to any address, postage paid, on receipt of price by the publisher.

J. G. CUPPLES, 250 Boylston St.,
BOSTON.

NEW FICTION.

The Chevalier of Pensieri-Vani; Together
with Frequent References to the Prorege of Arcopia. By
HENRY B. FULLER. Half binding, $1.25; paper, 50 cents.

The exquisite pleasure this book has given me.—CHARLES
ELIOT NORTON.

A precious book. . . It tastes of genius. — JAMES RUS-
SELL LOWELL.

A new departure, really new. — *Literary World.*

Penelope's Web: A Novel of Italy. By OWEN
INNSLY, author of " Love Poems and Sonnets." *A bit
of exquisite prose (the first) from Miss Jennison, whose
" Love Poems and Sonnets" went through so many editions.*
12mo, cloth, $1.50.

Stray Leaves from Newport: A Book of Fan-
cies. By Mrs. WILLIAM LAMONT WHEELER. Illustrated.
Finely printed, and most beautifully bound in tapestry,
white and gold. 16mo, cloth, $1.50; paper, 50 cents.
Fourth Edition.

By far the most popular book published upon America's
aristocratic resort ; written, too, by one of its leaders.

Something About Joe Cummings; or, A Son of
a Squaw in Search of a Mother. 12mo, cloth, $1.50.

A rough and ready story of the New South-west; not
vulgar, but strong, with a good deal of local color in it.

Eastward : or, a Buddhist Lover. By L. K. H.
12mo, cloth, $1.50.

Sure to please those who concur with SYDNEY SMITH as
to the meaning of *doxy.*

Hiero-Salem : The Vision of Peace. By E. L.
MASON. Illustrated. *A curious and remarkable novel,
interesting to those investigating Buddhism, Theosophy and
the position of woman.* Square 12mo, 508 pages, cloth, $2.00.

Fellow Travellers: A Story. By EDWARD
FULLER. 12mo, 341 pages, cloth, $1.00.

A brilliantly written novel, depicting New England life,
customs and manners, at the present time.

*Mailed, to any address, postage paid, on receipt of price by
the publisher.*

J. G. CUPPLES, 250 Boylston St.,
BOSTON.

NEW POETRY.

A Poet's Last Songs. Poems by the late HENRY
BERNARD CARPENTER, with introduction by JAMES JEFFREY
ROCHE, and portrait. 16mo, unique binding, $1.00.

This little volume is all that remains to us of the many-
gifted man who came to Boston a few years ago, a stranger and
unheralded, and took his place among her best poets and
orators by the right divine of genius.

Letter and Spirit. By A. M. RICHARDS.
By the wife of the celebrated American artist, WILLIAM T.
RICHARDS. Psychological and devotional in character,
and taking a high rank in American poetry. Square 12mo,
unique binding, $1.50.

No common, thoughtless verse-maker could produce, in
this most difficult form of the sonnet, such thoughtful and
exalted religious sentiments. — *Phila. Press.*

Letter and Spirit is a book to be studied and treasured. —
Boston Advertiser.

An admirable command over the difficulties of the sonnet is
shown. — *Gazette*, Boston.

Margaret and the Singer's Story. By EFFIE
DOUGLASS PUTNAM. *Second Edition.* 16mo, white cloth,
$1.25.

Graceful verses in the style of Miss Proctor, by one of
the same faith : namely, a Roman Catholic.

In Divers Tones. By HERBERT WOLCOTT
BOWEN. 16mo, half yellow satin, white sides, $1.25.
"Trifles light as a feather, caught in cunning forms."

Auld Scots Ballads, edited by ROBERT FORD.
Uniform with Auld Scots Humor. 1 vol., 300 pages, 16mo,
cloth. *Net, $1.75. Nearly ready.*

*Mailed, to any address, postage paid, on receipt of price by
the publisher.*

J. G. CUPPLES, 250 Boylston St.,
BOSTON.

RECENT AMERICANA.

Paul Revere: A Biography. By ELBRIDGE
HENRY GOSS.
Embellished with illustrations, comprising portraits, historical scenes, old and quaint localities, views of colonial streets and buildings, reproductions of curious and obsolete cuts, including many of Paul Revere's own caricatures and engravings, etc., etc., executed as photo-gravures, etchings, and woodcuts, many of them printed in colors. *Nearly ready.* 2 vols., 8vo, cloth, $6.00; large paper, $10.00.

Porter's Boston. Forty full-page, and over fifty smaller illustrations, by GEORGE R. TOLMAN. *2d edition.* 1 vol., large quarto, half sealskin, $6.00.
A few copies of the exceedingly scarce first edition can be had by direct application to the publisher, specially bound in half calf extra, for $9.00 net.

The Diary of Samuel Sewall, 1674-1729.
Edited by DR. G. E. ELLIS, W. H. WHITMORE, H. W. TORREY and JAMES RUSSELL LOWELL. With index of names, places and events. 3 vols., large 8vo. *Net,* $10.00.
This is a complete copy (printed at the University Press) of the famous diary of Chief Justice Sewall, the manuscript of which is one of the treasures of the Massachusetts Historical Society. It abounds in wit, humor and wisdom, and is *rich* in reference to names of early American families.

Acts of the Anti-Slavery Apostles. By PARKER
PILLSBURY. 12mo, 503 pages, cloth. *Net,* $2.00.
An authoritative and comprehensive work by one of the original leaders in the anti-slavery movement; not stereotyped and, as few copies remain for sale, it is certain to become an exceedingly scarce book.

Life of Admiral Sir Isaac Coffin, Baronet: His
English and American Ancestors. By Thomas C. Amory. With portrait. Large 8vo. *Net,* $1.50.
An elaborate biography of one of Nantucket's most famous sons, who rose to high rank in the British navy, and afterwards founded the celebrated Coffin schools in his native island. Interesting not only to members of the Coffin family, but to genealogists.

Mailed, to any address, postage paid, on receipt of price by the publisher.

J. G. CUPPLES, 250 Boylston St.,
BOSTON.

www.ingramcontent.com/pod-product-compliance
Lightning Source LLC
Chambersburg PA
CBHW020549270326
41927CB00006B/781